" The Poet's Perspective"

CYCLES

OF

LIFE

Poetry Plus Publishing
P.O. Box 365
Bangor, MI. 49013

THE POET'S PERSPECTIVE; "CYCLES OF LIFE"
Copyright© by Charles Edward Peterson, Sr.

For information please contact:

Poetry Plus Publishing
P.O. Box 365
Bangor, MI. 49013

Design and layout by RJ's Printing, LLC
in collaboration with Season Press, LLC

For more information regarding this author, go to **Spotify,** and look up **"THE POET SPEAKS,"** or look him up on **"You Tube,"** under **Charles E. Peterson Sr..** To schedule **speaking engagements** please contact: **theepoetspks@gmail. com (we go to Schools, Colleges, Churches, Christian Youth Camps, Senior Citizen Homes, and businesses, Etc.. Some of the topics we recite and focus on are, Drugs, Guns, and Alcohol, Afro - American History, Societies Role, Justice & Legality, Dreams & Goals, Success, Cancer awareness Groups, and the battle against Cancer."**

Re-veiwers: Please forward 2 Copies, to review to:

ISBN: 978-0-9772541-5-6

POETRY PLUS PUBLISHING
60407 M- 43 Hwy.
Bangor, Mi. 49013

To contact Charles Edward Peterson, Sr. directly email:
theepoetspks@gmail.com

Printed in the United States of America;

Intro:

From but a seed are our lives fulfilled

We live to die to live, our fates are sealed

So soil and seed intertwine

Bound by a cycle of marriage and time

Cycle ending always beginning anew

All from a seed that took root and grew

So from death we shall live again

Sown with yet reaped pure of sin... "SEED"

"Cycle ending always beginning anew"...

One of many:

"CYCLES OF LIFE"

"SUNRISE"

I once read a quote by Charles E. Peterson Sr., (also known as "Thee, or The Poet") that said; I want to write poetry that will open the eyes of the children of man before they are harvested by minds of destruction," end of quote.

With his new book of poetry, "Cycles of Life," "Thee Poet" has not only written
poetry to open our eyes but to also open our minds, our hearts, and our souls.

I met and became friends with The Poet during the early 90's. We both were still trying to find our "voices" as poets. What impressed me then about Charles was his seriousness about writing poetry. His commitment to wanting to be a voice to be heard, a voice that not only speaks to the people but a voice that also speaks for the people. I'm still impressed by that.

The Poet has taken his thoughts and feelings and molded them into words that have become a voice that speaks in rhythm and rhyme. His poetry gives voice to
intimate associations with life.

With the turning of each page of Cycles of Life, Charles E. Peterson, Sr. takes us on an emotional ride that looks deep into the struggles, the joys, the pains, the pride and the triumphs that we face in life. He also gives us encouragement, understanding, strength, and hope.

As we read the words of The Poet they penetrate deep into our very being to draw out our own memories, fears, dreams, and feelings. They resonate deep within us to bring out some type of emotional response.

The Poet has indeed found his voice and it can be heard loud and clear. Behold, Thee Poet speaks to us and it will serve us all well to listen.

Buddy Hannah
Poet/Playwright

ACKNOWLEDGEMENTS

First giving honor to God and the true author of all that I am blessed with to create and share. I thank God for blessings me with the ability to apply spiritual gifts with talent and it's been said, "work wonders with His words." I thank Him, for giving me poetic messages, and analogies, which allow me to focus on, pin-point, and elaborate on many issues that are relative in today's society.

To the loving memory of my Mother (The Old Girl), Mrs. Rosielee Peterson, and my Father, Mr. Willie Edward Lee Moses Malachi Peterson (The Old Man), yet love you both. Together they planted the seeds of family values and strength of conviction which gave me a thirst to fulfill the responsibilities passed on. And also instilled a tenacity laced with strength of character, entwined in a *Can Do Spirit*.

I would like to thank my wife, Joyce Lee (whom I Love with a Passion), who has encouraged, inspires, and completes me. I thank her for understanding I need just a few more minutes or so to write, and I'll be to bed soon (maybe).

I thank my brothers Salih (Rasmiah), Oscar (Linda) Clarence(deceased) (Rosa), Ulysses (Linda), Benjamin (deceased) and my only sister May (Dwayne). I would also like to thank a special cousin Selena (J.C.- deceased).

I love you all unconditionally. You have all helped to fulfill my dream spiritually, mentally, and or physically.

Fate led me to becoming a single parent, I would not have chosen this path, but through "The Cycle Of Life," I was able to endure this test of time. For all the wisdom my parents taught me and exemplified, flowed from me far beyond my recognition, until years down this winding road. As I sought to raise my children Anita Shari, Tanisha Charlotte, and Charles Edward Jr., in the midst of my efforts I was led back in God's Hands. But before I turned back to find God, I found myself lost in "SOCITIES ROLE," angry, vengeful, and climbing out of a deep pit, with three children who needed a father a daddy, not the man that I had become unbeknownst to them and many others. But I found myself in part between the lines of creativity that over the years flowed and helped heal a wounded spirit. For the seed planted in my youth constantly echoed "The Cycle," "Les We Forget." May this last paragraph be encouragement to many who are going through "SOCIETY'S ROLE," "time heals, things change, bad times don't last always, and "SUCCESS" CAN BE FOUND DOWN AVENUES YOU'RE YET TO SEE."

I give a special thanks to all those who have assisted or encouraged me along the way including my church family. Thank you and may God Bless.

And as always I give honor to *God* for all *His* gifts and over fifty years of creativity. Surely ink flows through my veins, in *His* name.

Charles Edward Peterson, Sr.-The Poet

I DEDICATE:

I Humbly Dedicate, {The Poet's Perspective on} "THE CYCLE OF LIFE," to all Poets and Writers who take their gifts and talents to the actual arena of life SEEKING, AWARENESS, CHANGE, DOCUMINTATION, HISTORIC ILLUMINATION, and or are striving to "BRIDGE A GAP" an EVER WIDENING, VOLITILE, "SEPERATING GAP." Know that you are relevant in times like these, "not by happenstance but by NECESSITY."

What cause or issue will you use your Gift(s), to BRING AWARENESS to or SUPPORT?

ROE V WADE - SAME SEX MARRIAGE - CRITICAL RACE THEORY-PRISON REFORM- POLITICS - & OR, VOTER SUPPRESSION

COVID 19 - HOMLESSNESS - CLIMATE CHANGE - MINIMUM WAGE - GAS PRICES - FOOD, INFLATION & OR RECESSION

MASS SHOOTINGS - POLICE BRUTALITY - RACIAL TENSION - FAKE NEWS - DIVERSITY & INCLUSION - THE THREAT OF WAR & THE INSURRECTION

A NATION THAT SEEMS TO HAVE TURNED FROM AND INSCRIBED NOTATION "IN GOD WE TRUST," AND A WORLD THAT IS IN DIRE NEED OF CHANGE, AND THE RESTORATION OF OUR FAITH, IN HIS INTERCESSION.

"WHAT PURPOSE OR CAUSE WOULD YOU HELP THE CHILDERN OF MAN ON YOUR MORALS AND INTEGRITY DARE TO STAND?" THE POET.

To
Van Buren
District Library
(Covert Branch)

God Bless, and may this
gift make a difference in the lpes
of our Community.

"Behold the Blessing of
"The Poet."

Dea Charles Potter Jr.
"The Poet."
9/11/2023

(And then comes)."The Poet."

Charles Edward Peterson Sr., was born on May 9, 1950 (Fourth son of seven sons and one daughter), to Rosielee and Willie, Edward Lee Moses Malachi, Peterson. After high school he married, seven years later, he became a single Parent, of two Daughters and a Son, (by the Grace of God and the "village" he raised three healthy children), and later, raised a Grandson.

The Poet is a civil rights activist, community leader and humanitarian. A former Union President (two terms), a trustee at V.B.U. Civic Org., the Grand Marshall of his communities 150th year Parade, his community service, also includes reciting poetry at a correctional facility, Christian youth camps, civic organizations, schools, colleges, and participation in marches (the second Million Man March in Wash. D.C., & the Thousand Man March in Kalamazoo, Mi.) for unity awareness and atonement. He has also been a mentor at his Alma mater, is very active in his church as the Deacon Chair., Sunday School Superintendent, teacher (men's class), and male chorus member. He's a former District Layman's President, for the Chain Lake District (the Oldest District in Mi. 179 years,) & presently the Vice President @ Large, of the Wolverine State Laymen's Ministry.
He proudly holds the Rank of Black Belt in the Martial Arts, plays Chess, says he has a "degree in "Bid whist - ology," likes bowling, Fishing, and is an avid Golfer. That "he says" makes him a little talented, but his "Gift and Passion is," "Poetry and Creative Writing." He has written three books of poetry, and with the "CYCLES OF LIFE," three books of Poetry and Philosophy, under the banner of, "THE POET'S PERSPECTIVE." "The Poet" has been writings over fifty- five year. "The Poet" is but "a voice crying in the wilderness," trying to *open the eyes of the children of man, before they are harvested by minds of destruction.*

"The Poet."

V

****

Most acrostics are to be read as
The Last Sentence of The Poem
(or Work).

"CYCLES OF LIFE"

... Generation after generation have passed it on
That wisdom and knowledge that makes us strong
And the age of "hope and change" has finally arrived
Acknowledging that the "Dream and Vision" yet survive
Surely there is more to do and more to overcome
Like personally informing our children
What we came through and where we came from
That we've come a long way from where we begun
And that they "MUST"continue to protect what's been won
For where we are was seen in "Dreams and Visions" long long
ago.
And many sacrificed life, blood, sweat, and tears to make it so...

"THE CYCLE"
Charles Edward Peterson, Sr.

It's a legacy passed on by the "old warriors" devout, stun gent, oaken, women and men. It's a harmony that can only be amplified by the whisper of the wind. It's a privileged anointing seeking atonement that "erupts" deep down within. It's an agonizing yet, resounding, remnant, that bond "now to then":

Boom, bubaboom, bubaboom, bubaboom, ba
Boom, bubaboom, bubaboom, bubaboom
Boom, bubaboom, bubaboom, bubaboom, ba
Boom, bubaboom, bubaboom, bubaboom

"THE BEAT"

Moving to the rhythm of a tempo unheard

To a language beyond the spoken word

The language that's universal, known the world around

Beat that's beating where the roots of your dreams are found

Of all the things which are essential to life

A pulse that derived through hardship and strife

Different because everyone isn't privileged to the sound

Drummer soul and body intertwined in an ancient rhythm profound

"The Beat," it's what solidifies the village, and unifies "the tribe." It's that taut unbreakable strand that kept us alive that "gut wrenching hope" that endured "the test of time." It was that "monumental effort of endurance," their mountain to climb. If you're privileged, and you listen, it's "your rhythm of life." Not listening will lead you back, to a life, of "hardship and strife."

"A pulse that derived through hardship and strife"

What was "LOST" in the Abduction, in the Journey, in the ineffable enslavement, during the centuries, has been highlighted, and expounded on, as that which was and is the endurance, strength, and a testament, of a people, for surviving that which was:

"LOST"

LOST ROOTS, LOST LINAGE, LOST FAMILY,

LOST PRIDE, LOST HONOR, LOST IDENITY,

LOST PEOPLE, LOST HERITAGE, LOST COUNTRY,

LOST CULTURE, LOST LANGUAGE, LOST MEMORY,

LOST FREEDOM, LOST LIVES, LOST LEGACY

ALL LOST-N-HIS-STORY.

BUT NEVER LOST,

"HOPE," "VISION," NOR "THE BEAT"
Boom, bubaboom, bubaboom, bubaboom, ba

of "OUR ANCESTRY"

Surely the strength and endurance, verifies the character and core of a people, but the true "testament" of the people rest in their
"FAITH, HOPE, AND HUMANITY."

We've come a long ways from the Motherland to the Land of Milk and Honey.
But the completion of the span across the waters was only the beginning of our Journey.

"AFRICA"

What more can be said of Africa that has not been said many, many, times before.
How many times have it been questioned, the "ineffable demeanor of man"

How many trips did it take, to secure the amount of slaves it took, TO

Build the foundation of this great Nation, on which we stand

How many souls were lost, and the question is asked again.
For it yet fuels the fire (in part) of man's inhumanity towards men

How do we douse this fire that yet burns in many a mind and heart
That more often sets this Great Nation aback, and yet pulls it apart... AFRICA

The Motherland, from where many roots were severed and lost
From, where many seeds drifted to far and distant shores

Rooted, and grew up weary of home, yet "stout and strong"
While the life giving blood seeped and more often, poured from their pores
Where, the longing if measured in blood sweat and tears could measure the "mighty
Niles Flow, where the mind wonders of a severed linage it, no longer know... The
Mother Land
Do you ever dream wrestles dreams of lost children from a time gone by
Do you ever kneel, by your awesome shores weeping, weeping and wonder why
Have you ever considered what we could have built together "stout and strong"
If somehow we could've banned together, to deny histories ineffable wrong AFRICA
We have become seeds of many Nations, called by many names
Cubans, Haitians, Jamaicans, to name a few, all from a severed linage, yet one in the
same
So what more can I say of Africa, living in the "land of the free,"
called African, Nigger, Negro, Colored, Black, names documenting our history,

Except that, "Your Seed, has become a Mighty Tree," "well rooted in the land" Known
far and wide, for creativity, endurance, perseverance, soul food, righteousness, an as
an "Afro-American"

"AFRICA"

Did I mention that "the journey" was only the beginning of "our journey"? The shackles, the plantations of cotton fields and tobacco fields, and all those who soldiered, in that era known and unknown, bound and free, wrote on a page of our history. For they set the stage, and prepared a way for men like, The Rev. Dr. Martin Luther King Jr., Malcom X, Judge Thurgood Marshall, Joe Louis, Mohammad Ali, and President Barrack Obama. For, they stood on the shoulders of "Giants," as we must, to align "The Cycle" of the past, with the seeds of the future.

"THE MOTHER LAND"

"Freedom "O" Freedom," how long has it been, what an awesome awaking to see you again. What if you were awakened to your long awaited desire, and before you could relish in the moment, it was snatched away. And you found yourself "hostage" to your former reality, "woe to the woe." You are in need of emancipation again.

GENERAL ORDER #3 - (6/19/1865)

The Emancipation Proclamation issued by Pres. Abraham Lincoln, On January 1, 1863

Was a promissory note of Freedom, it proclaimed the end of slavery

But for those yet, enslaved in Galveston, Texas it proved to be but a counterfeit note

For, for two and a half years it wasn't worth the paper on which it was wrote

For many Confederate rebels held former slaves hostage not honoring the decree

It took a U.S. Major General with 1800 troops, on June 19, 1865 executing General Order # 3.

It took the execution of Marshal Law, to force the rebels to comply, And a battle did begin

It sounded the final curtain call for slavery and established Juneteenth's origin.

The war was finally over, the Emancipation Proclamation issued, and The 13th Amendment ratified

But, because of those who would not comply

Some only tasted Freedom, before they died.

But because of the efforts of freedmen and lobbyist, (in part)

Came, GENERAL ORDER #3

Mandating by the Chief Executive, of the United States, that

"ALL SLAVES ARE FREE"

That time has passed for many,

But I'm reminded and I come to remind you that history often repeats itself

Maybe not always on the grander scale

But knowing that it yet makes be somewhat weary within myself

For many of our young women and children are subjected to trafficking

And our yet being enslaved

Many of our people are subjected to "systemic racism," and are often" unjustly"

Incarcerated in "a prison system" that many equate to "legal slavery"

Let the truth be known, that system is in dire need of change

For the time of slavery in these often Un-United States hasn't altogether gone

So Juneteenth is a celebration of freedom, twice denied

Let's celebrate it also, as a reminder of a threat, that yet abide

In our celebrating we should never, never, never take for granite being free

And come together, and work together, and pray together, and reason together,

And stand together, to protect and fortify our freedom remembering,

GENERAL ORDER #3

That time has passed, that t-i-m-e has passed, "ooor,"has it? if not, why not? Don't you believe that one of the most "heinous crimes" known to man deserves the greatest deterrent, that it never be allowed again in society.

What will it take to overcome that which is systemic, that is bred into the children of man?

How can we alleviate, let alone continue to endure the trials of an unjust court. As we continue seeing a nation reaching beyond its borders, seeking to orchestrate the need for democracy around the world. As we continue:

ENDURING & OVERCOMING

We've overcome many obstacles

Come up against many trials along the way

A monument to our resilience

Long suffering forever and a day

Way overshadowed by bigotry

But we're yet filled with great anticipation

We've withstood racism and oppression

Got this far by fighting to overcome discrimination

A plague that's common from generation to generation

Long implanted by hatred, prejudice, and fear

Way of life always threatened

To survive we must remember and build on what got us here

Go forward rebuilding a foundation, that can sustain a diverse nation

In many ways, "we have scaled the mountain of injustice" and verified the need for change. But the "roots of racism" runs deep and must be extracted, before we can become "one nation under God."

That first step, that inner questioning, that often wondering light at the end of the tunnel mentality, because this is not a weekend getaway, or a short trek, looking at the scope and span of it, it can only be deemed,

THE JOURNEY

The quest to achieve beyond, the

Journey that begun with a single step

Is filled with challenges, that

Often ensure an inner commitment be kept

More times than not it makes you align with what's

Important, to the fulfillment of your quest

Then to focus on the latter

The end results of how you mature, in pursuit of your

Destination, is often more so what matter

As always on any journey there are many alternate routes and events that may detour us from our original course. And we often have to adjust our timelines, reroute and realign ourselves to reach our destination. But what we learn about ourselves in between that first step, and our destination, is often more what we remember about "t h e j o u r n e y."

9

Where is the bottom line of our shame? Could it be or was it the Lack of appreciation or the Lack of transparence, to the LACKS family.

"HENRIETTA LACKS" - (APPRECIATION DAY)

When someone is "Blessed" to impact society in a special way

There should be on the Calendar a declared and dedicated day

So that the world comes to appreciate, acknowledge, and acclaim the same

Let's, start by ESTABLISHING A HOLIDAY, in HENRIETTA LACK'S NAME,

Henrietta Lacks, Immortal Cells

Has aided mankind around the world

The discovery of these cells was the first of their kind

They revolutionized medical research, and established the "HeLa Line"

The declaration of this holiday should not be postponed

Because her Immortal Cells were so revolutionary, they were even "cloned"

Often we have gone back "posthumously" to give "Medals Of Honor" that were due

We shouldn't hesitate for this one is L.A.C.K.I.N.G. and long overdue

Considering how her Immortal Cells are yet, aiding mankind

You need to join me with "ONE VOICE" and say

"WE NEED TO DECLARE AND DEDICATE AUGUST 1, AS HENRIETTA LACKS, APPRECIATION DAY".

How do we begin to right a wrong?

That, which was buried for so long

By lifting it from the dust, in dedication

Acknowledgement, elevation, and education

Billions of billions of dollars have been made

Millions of millions of lives may have been saved

Hundreds of her family members may have gone to the grave

Some who possibly wasn't allowed HeLa cells, that their lives could be saved

MRS. HENRIETTA LACKS - (1920-1951)

When is closing our eyes, hiding our hands, and suppressing a truth that benefits our nation and the world, worthy of something that we do?

HENRIETTA LACKS
The:
Mother
Of
Modren
Medicine

you can just call her
"M.OM.M."

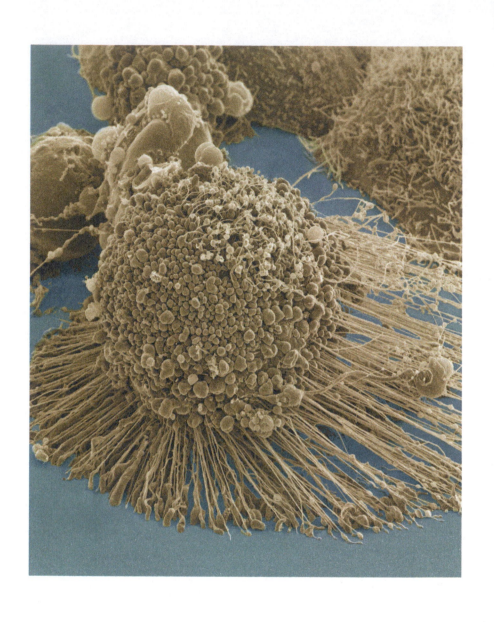

"HELA CELLS"

L.A.C.K.I.N.G.

What is considered L.A.C.K.I.N.G.? Well it's often found in situations where an action is found legal but is unjust, when someone cold heartedly omits those who are entitled, when others are allowed to profit from another's life ending sacrifice. You are found guilty of, L.A.C.K.I.N.G., when you can add any of these to the start of what's L.A.C.K.I.N.G. (when/ when it's/when some-one's/when it's considered/when you.)

Legal but Unjust

A person's place in history is found under an unmarked grave

Contributions because of race, color, gender, or creed are hidden

Keeping all the benefits from the next generation of kin, is deemed ok

Immortality is suppressed by LACKS, of Integrity

Neglect to inform, acknowledge, or compensate family, is known, and yet acceptable

Gain is selfishly obtained from someone else's contribution that ended in their death

So be it declared that society is guilty of L.A.C.K.I.N.G., to the deceased, MRS. HENRETTA LACKS, to her Kindred, and to Society for not being informed of her "IMMORTAL CONTRIBUTION, that has been an aid to saving lives and preserving the quality of life, not only in this Great Nation, but around The World.

Did you miss it? You know a whole lot of people have. They understand and understood the essence of "The Dream," but didn't see the dept or full significance of "The Vision."

"THE VISION"

He moved to the beat of a different drummer

For none violence was his weapon of choice.

He tried to hold the system accountable to its creed

"We hold these truths to be self- evidence

That all men are created equal." it was a means to succeed.

He marched,he spoke, he sat in joining hand and heart

Striving to make a difference now we must do our part

His legacy was a "dream," a "dream," only in part fulfilled

For I often wonder how much more he could have accomplished if he hadn't been killed

He scalded a mountain in a "Vision" and was blessed to see the other side

It enhanced his decision to go forward with **"The Dream"**

Even though, even though in **"The Vision"** he had died.

For I can remember hearing him say **"even though I may not, even though I may not**

We as a people shall see the promise land"

The seeds of equality, balance and justice has long been planted

But racism, prejudices, and hatred are the weeds that bind

And its been a long row to hoe for the many known and unknown soldiers

14

Trying to eradicate a hardened heart, mind, and a spirit defying

But, the fruits of his and many known and unknown soldier's

Labors, has finally come in range

For because of their keeping "HOPE ALIVE"

We're now in the age of "BELIEVING AND CHANGE"

Surely he marched to the beat of a "different drummer"

They assassinated "THE DRUMMER" but we're here to verify that "The Beat" goes on

Surely he was "A DRUM MAJOR FOR JUSTICE"

So to celebrate his birthday is only justified

I just wanted to get that clarified

For history has verified "he" was blessed gifted and qualified

And we as a people (and many others) come together "gratified"

Because we know that he was "bona fide."

When you remember "The Dream," remember "The Vision," understand in part the true significance of his decision to "willingly" go forward with "The Dream." And that he was but one example why each generation owes the previous generation. For we reap the rewards of their era and efforts. And their Dreams, Hopes, and Visions are placed in our care.

"For history has verified "he" was blessed gifted and qualified"

"Change will not come if we wait for some other person or some other time. We are the ones we've been waiting for. We are the change that we seek."

Barack Obama

Have you ever witnessed the dawn of a new day,
Or been at the forefront of history in the making?
How awesome it was to witness the mass unity, of the majority,
of the American people, uniting at the polls, to elect the first
Black, or Afro -
American, President of the United States. President, elect
Barack

"OBAMA"

It was the Third of January on a new year's dawn
When for "Senator Barack Obama," Iowa was won
Our nation and histories first
He certified and verified that with hope comes change
And that if you'd but believe things would no longer be the same
No longer the same old conclusions
From often a bought and paid for machine
A cold and callous entity
That destroys the American dream
With hope he proved that we as Americans could stand as one
And not be divided by red and blue as the machine had done
With hope he proved that all the small fractions could unite
And with a lot of small contributions win the battle
Not just put up a good fight
And it came by belief for the white, yellow, black, brown, and red
Came together as one and said, to the machine, your way is through
Our voices and votes represent the true America
The "melting pot," the Red, White, and the Blue
And if you'll believe and surly lend an ear
You'll know that change isn't only possible
But that "change" is finally here

Awesome, I will never forget how we came together on one accord.
How we put aside our differences and stepped out on faith and
believed in a challenge to change the imbalance of the system. But
true change comes from a broad clearing of stumbling blocks, with
"individual" as well as "mass" participation. Because as always the
true fight is down in the trenches or behind closed doors.

With hope he proved that we as Americans could stand as one

I can't say that it was like the "domino effect because in that process you stage a predictable end.
But to get caught up and watch the process constantly reveal the unexpected, with unexpected states, votes saying he should be elected.
I knew we had come along ways, but I never thought it would happen:

"IN MY LIFE TIME"

I look back to where I never saw it coming
Never believed all the media's buzz and humming

Thought it was as an unattainable reality in my mind
It was something to view on the big screen for a future time

Would possible happen in my grandchildren's age
Happen because of a "domino effect" on a "contrary" stage

At least through a lot more heartache and pain
Least with a more gradual process of struggle and gain

Not something I would be able to see unfold right before my eyes
In a fashion that would take the "world" by surprise

My generation I'm sure thought it was out of range, having a
Lifetime of believing and hoping our children would see the change

May "God" not let "wonders" ever cease. just when we think we've got this living on earth thing figured out, the unexpected lets us know, that we're not running it,we're just running around in it.

I NEVER THOUGHT IT WOULD HAPPEN
        AT LEAST NOT IN MY LIFE TIME....

18

"When you see something that is not right,

You have a moral obligation to do

something."

Mr. John L. Lewis
(Congressman)

"GOOD TROUBLE"

To stand together, march together, speak out together, and serve and work as citizens within the bounds of the law, is "true patriotism." To encourage the system, to honor its written Declaration concerning Liberty, "which is the state of not being imprisoned or enslaved," "the state of being free within society." To seek it, by taking a stand in protest, let it be deemed: "GOOD TROUBLE"

Given a history where giving up is not an option

Oppressed people shall always seek freedom and equality

Our only hope is to stand up against systemic racism

Dilemma being that some believe, freedom is but an ideology

Time yet echoes "injustice for one is injustice for all"

Requiring us to come together, and stand against a racist society

Our meager successes, never separates "the tree from the root"

Unrest reveals it matters not, our service, nor contributions in history

Because of a presumed racial superiority, that inflames a nation

Life is already an uphill battle, but we must standup against bigotry

Echoing, is an ineffable demeanor, and a failed political apostasy

To stand together as "one society means" to "uphold" that which has been "ordained and established," the "posterity," (of all future generations of people)."

Unrest reveals a waning patriotism being replaced with political apostasy

G.O.O.D.T.R.O.U.B.L.E.

The carryover of a life time of misery and forced servitude, left many of the Old Warriors" bound in a viscous cycle, a cycle of rising and falling, striving and struggling, from generation to generation. And as many of the "old warriors" were then, many today are, "sick and tire of being:

"SICK AND TIRED"

I'm almost at my wits end - seeing it over and over again

Sick of the infighting, masquerade, and trying to pretend

And always having to be the one to go that extra mile

Tired of that masked fake and phony smile

Of that firm hearty, handshake that extends deceit

Being cultivated by so many that you greet

Sick of those who claim but actually don't really care

And those who promise but once elevated can't see you from there

Tired, tired, tired, of being sick and tired.

How amazing is it that at times, as far as we've come, it often seems that time has stood still. Those aware of the actual struggle, who are and were attached or submerged in the grips of the times, measure the similarities of yesterday and today. And every now and then when another caption of "man's inhumanity to man" comes across the airways or appears on the screen, even though you see that "oaken spirit" in them, you can see in their eyes they are tired, tired, tired.

22

It has been grafted in our history, bound to our efforts to rise up from the shadows, of oppression. "Equality is not a mark that can't be achieved, but possible one that is seemingly being "slept" by, **"TOO MANY OF US"**

"TOO MANY OF US"

There has always been direction

Are presently those who know the way

Far back as I can remember, we were told

Too take heed, and prepare for the day

Many sacrifices were made on our behalves

Of which in return a lot was expected of us

Us, and the generations to come can't be found

Sleeping in the time of reaping and trust

In a time where opportunity flourishes

A time when dreams and visions align

Dangerous is it to take our liberties for granted

Time yet warns of the "ineffable" demeanor of mankind.

It has been spoken of by the "Old Warriors" who suffered through some of the harshest of times, that we are trusted to "protect what's been gained." And to always remember that, "history often repeats itself."

"IF THERE IS NO STRUGGLE THERE IS NO PROGRESS."

Frederick Douglass: *FREEDOM FIGHTER*

Some of you don't know about, outdoor water pumps (that you have to prime), pot belly stoves, or having to eat wild game. But it was all a part of "the struggle," "back in the day," And although many have been blessed to reach great heights, far beyond that day and time. I come to remind you that, there are those who are still:

"STRUGGLING"

The times have changed for many

Struggle seems truly a thing of the past

Isn't something you face day to day

Over in another time and place at last

Because of the sacrifices that others made

You're blessed with success and you're not alone

No time like the present to let the truth be known

Longer it's unspoken the longer it'll go on

Struggling isn't over, just because your struggle is gone

I remember someone close to me who didn't realize that the country was in a recession. Had got comfortable in the blessing they were receiving and thought life was good across the board. They had a moment. It happens probably more than you think. So get beyond the moment, and back to the reality of the day.

"Struggling isn't over, because you're no longer struggling."

At this point in time I'm a laboring dream, a fading vision, a "countless sacrifice" transcending the ages. I represent all the blood, sweat, and tears that have been shed throughout the years that have brought you to this time of "opportunity and potential." I am the voice of the "old warriors" bond and free. I represent that "small wee voice that roars in your spirit." Urging you to look beyond your own meager successes and realize they were achieved in part by "sacrifices transcending the ages." So when you get over "the moment," remember we are depending on you to maintain:

"THE CYCLE"

Those who reap the fruits of today

Owe those who sowed the seeds of yesterday

To prepare a harvest for the children of tomorrow

That their age in time will be filled with less sorrow

For our children, and children's, children

Will lead in the technology age

Where they can text, tweet, or create on a "3 dimensional stage"

Where the doors of opportunity are opened wide

And our young people are just beginning to stride

For their age will be as a warp in time

Creating and discovering new "degrees" to challenge the mind

Reaching out to and beyond the stars new wisdom to find

Discovering new challenges to gather and bind

For generation after generation have passed it on

That wisdom and knowledge that makes us strong

And the age of "hope and change" has finally arrived

Acknowledging that the "Dream and Vision" yet survive

Surely there is more to do and more to overcome

Like personally informing our children

What we've come through and where we came from

That we've come a long ways from where we begun

And that they must, continue to protect, what's been won

For where we are was seen in "Dreams and Visions" long, long ago

And many, many, sacrificed life, blood, sweat, and tears to make it so

And as you profit from, build upon, and protect what's been gained

The "cycle" through your efforts will be maintained

And as you strive for success to better self and the present humanity

Don't forget the debt you owe to the past and future society

And to those who've become, and to those who becomes

Tight fisted with what you own

"Remember," most of your life "you've reaped what you haven't sown."

And every day is another test of time. An as life often teaches, there are some test we can't afford to fail. It takes a whole village to raise a child means that we need to get back to looking out for each other. "The needs of the many..."

"Remember," most of your life "you've reaped what you haven't sown."

What A travesty, an unbelievable display of the misuse of authority, which left a people and a nation proclaiming:

"I CAN'T BREATHE"

I couldn't believe my eyes, as I watched in frustration

Can't see how by it being filmed they didn't defuse the situation

Breathe, the breath of life, each as though it were your last inhalation

Black People, for being Black is as a crime, in our nation

Lives are severed from our people, like our lives are as an abomination

Matter not our contribution, service, or dedication

Get you to the back of the bus, is still their expectation

Your lack of because of "white privilege," is not in the equation

Knee of protest, hands up don't shoot, the new norm, or inclination

Off, when the cameras are off, the police get off, it's a legal violation

My People, we've survived our bodies and minds, being bound for generations

Neck and neck, with change, bound by struggles, future hopes, and a present determination

How did we get to this point, where even if we are innocent and being victimized, we feel threatened, threatened to the point of filming the police when they come, and to call them, for some, is the last result.

I CAN'T BREATHE, BLACK LIVES MATTER; GET YOUR KNEE OF MY NECK.

Sometimes we don't give credit where it's due, other times we for whatever reason don't listen to what we hear. But often the worst thing we can do is to not believe our own eyes. As we visualize a:

PORTRAYED IMAGE

When it's verified by their actions or

Someone stands on a platform stating what they are about

Shows they are dedicated to an unknown cause

You can't give them the benefit of the doubt

Who stands on their soapbox and expound that

They are here and in place by design

Are out spoken and clear in action and deed

Believe in it enough to give you a piece of their mind

Them, and their ideology could have you hanging from a limb

Blink em, rub em, use eye drops, but by all means when you have to see what you're looking at, look at what you see.

When Someone Shows You Who They are Believe Them!!!

It's like a vail over the eyes, and earmuffs over the ears, it's like that
constant barrage, of bad or deadly news that's horrible, but doesn't affect
you. So you brush off these often major atrocities, with a shrug of the
shoulder or a shake of the head, or a shallow exclamation, that leaves many:

"CLUELESS"

What a life to have lived not knowing in your midst

There were and are those who are systemically oppressed

To see the horrors of others day to day life

And not recognize that the system is unjust

What a remark to hear after another black youth

Is publicly murdered or lying near dead

That you had no clue it was this way

How you're oblivious of what goes on around you day to day

How you presumed you made it on your own

Not recognizing racism as the cause

Over more qualified minorities,

When it's clearly separate and unequal laws

How many have been silenced for standing up for what's right

For standing in the gap, fighting the good fight

Fear has been heightened and bigotry's on the rise

How prejudices and racism hinders compromise

How the leaders of the nation are in constant disarray

How those embolden question the letter of the law

Trying to convince us that on JANUARY SIX 2021,

We didn't see what we saw.

Ok, I get it; you get ten people witnessing the same incident you can come up with ten different scenarios of what just happened. But to live in a society where it's always happening somewhere, and not know, "humm."

Although we are in many ways still experiencing the aftershock of "911," like "ripples" echoing from shore to shore. And although retaliation came swift and strong, the fire smoldered but hasn't gone out. And that's why our "heightened sense of awareness" leaves us with a bitter taste for:

"THE FLAVOR OF THE DAY"

With war and destruction highlighting the six o'clock news

Those in charge spouting revenge and lighting a very short fuse

An alarming situation a terrible smoking gun

But someone must pay for what has been done

Terror is ever present it's certainly time to pray

For terrorism is the unfortunate "flavor of the day"

War on the home front what have they done

Somebody anybody everybody, call and (remember) 911

The near unimaginable has finally come to be

The thing only thought of in fiction has become reality

Our mighty shores couldn't protect from an enemy within

From another horrid effort of man's inhumanity to men

From a war never declared a cowardly act

Many victims and heroes die because of a sneak attack

There are no rules of engagement civilians are targets as well

The unexpected horror of the reality of a living hell

Many are suspected and suspicions run high

The enemy is often invisible to the naked eye

There's a heighten sense of awareness

The war of the world has finale struck home

We've deployed men our retaliation is strong

We took the war to the terrorist

Even though they died in the effort they made

Those that harbored and protected them are the ones that paid

They destroyed the towers but we towered over them

They awoke "the sleeping Giant" now they're out on a limb

Because the only thing he likes more than "peace and tranquility"

Is proving at the "art of war" he holds "a superiority"

I know, I know, I know that this is a very sensitive issue an there are those who haven't gotten over it and may never get over it. But, when do we interject that violence "begets" violence, and hate "begets" hate, and "if we keep doing the same thing..." and how about the healing process, and the effort it takes to close an open wound. And to not have others suffer or experience the same hurt or demise. I know to some there will never be a right time, but I guess if we can't work it out or won't forgive each other as fellow human beings, Then keep an eye to the sky (in more ways than one) ....

"Somebody, anybody, everybody, call and
(remember) 911"

It's an uphill battle, caused by an uneven battlefield; it's a moral dilemma that has hampered generations, founded on injustice and an alleged racial inferiority. An advantage known as:

THE EDGE

Why do you believe you hold an advantage

How can you justify others being bottlenecked in a wedge

Is it because of your wisdom or knowledge

That causes others to often teeter on the edge

Everyone that has ever crossed your path

Paid a cost, your history has documented and proclaimed

Reason why they nor we couldn't measure up

It was because you're given every advantage named

Victims throughout the annals of time

Insist that your edge is inhumane

Lives have been altered, and lost, the edge bears the blame

Everyone knows the answer like nepotism in the work place

Given such an unequal advantage you lead most every race

Even though many deny it, it's obvious why others teeter on the ledge

Even though it's not going to be fixed overnight, and shall possible take generations to change, by those who believe, that it and anything resembling it no matter what the color, divides and weakens our nation. But there is no better time than now, to plant the seeds of change.

The two are entwined in a constant give and take union
A heathy duet engaged in an awesome relevant two step
That stymie's a People **-WITHOUT -** *a vision*

Without Faith within Without

A destructive battle wages with A

Vision that's needed for a People

The journey is filled with calamity The

People walk in darkness, having no Vision

Perish for without direction and unity they'll Perish

Where there is division it weakens the created vision

Where the people are un- united, the stability, of the established

norm

Is weakened, and if not healed, perishes.

It's been said, "if you keep doing the same thing you've always done you'll keep getting the same thing you've always got." It's like being on a merry go round and although it appears that there's a thousand ways to exit, without stepping off into the mud. You're not only muddy, but muddy again, and in front of a crowd.

"CAN'T"

Can't see it

Can't see why

Can't see how

Couldn't see it then can't see it now

Can't see where it's going

Can't see where it's going to end

Couldn't see it from the beginning

Can't see it now couldn't see it then

Can't see the logic beyond the emotional drain

Can't see success beyond the physical strain

Can't see how to turn it all around

Can't see how to fix what's about torn down

Can't see all that needs to be rearranged

And

Can't see progress without change

It's been said, "if you keep doing the same thing you've always done, you'll keep getting the same thing you've always got." It's like being on a merry go round and although it appears that there's a thousand ways to exit, without stepping off into the mud. You're not only muddy, but muddy again, and in front of a crowd.

(Did I just do the same thing top and bottom?)

Can't see progress without change

As sure as it's a bad wind that rarely changes its direction, it's equally as bad, if you are bound by situation or circumstance, that's hampered by lack of progress, and fear of:

CHANGE

The clock is ticking

Time is winding down

Is there a sign of change?

Now the cry is evident world around

The meaning is awesome

Message is unique and sound

Is the darkest hour still just before day?

Clear your mind and it'll no longer be bound

There must be something done to defuse the ever ticking clock

Can more communication be the answer that the solution be found?

Be it known it was written that every man is his brother's keeper

No time like the present to recreate a system that's run aground

Progress can be obtained by reinstating justice for all

Without "justice" we can't be who we claim to be world renown

Change is constant, but indifference abound, unity must prevail in order to rebound

It's an awesome thing to see the light at the end of the tunnel, but find the closer you get to it, the farther away it becomes. And know that it's not just getting out of this tunnel that will make the difference, but finding out why the "light" keeps getting moved.

"The Time Is Now The Message Is Clear There Can Be No Progress Without Change."

Wouldn't you hate it, if when things were out of control; no one was held accountable for their actions. And there were no methods set in place to establish or reestablish a sense of a known normality. No form of justice or semblance of:

"ORDER"

Without rules and regulations there is no "Order"

Without "<u>Order</u>" there is chaos

With chaos comes anarchy and destruction

With anarchy and destruction comes the need

For rules and regulations

With rules and regulations

Comes "<u>Order</u>"

It's a "necessity", revolving in the midst of a "vicious circle of chaos." It's that answer that is sought after, when you make that call for help. In all phases of your need you want to somehow, someway, find or return things to "<u>Order.</u>"

You knew it would come to a vote, a highly opinionated nationally debated issue. And although no one agrees on the issues the majority agrees upon the "solutions." But no one seems to know quite how to get those "pivotal points" implemented into:

"RESOLUTIONS"

Those caught up often in the unbalanced scales of justice

Who yet believe in the principles set by the founding fathers

Make up the true majority of the present minority

Peaceful and lawful means are the avenues they pursue

Resolutions within the perimeters of the written law

Impossible is it to continue to obey "the laws' when those who

Make the laws "break the laws"

Violent is the ultimate response when rights are suppressed

Resolutions are often null and void in the midst of a state of unrest

Inevitable is the turmoil that entangles that which is unjust

As the war on words continue, and public opinion often spills out into the streets, and the system seems to at times stand firmly behind whatever version or form of "implementation," that is considered just or law. At times it seems, to some, as far as we've come, we're still not too far removed from the "fifties and sixties."

Those Who Make Peaceful Resolutions Impossible Make Violent Resolutions Inevitable.

Societies Role;

Relates to the past, present, and future, the seen and unseen, known and unknown, roles in life that we play Many being casted for us, and being "deduced" as the expected norm. It's a means to an end, and effort to segregate, a means to denigrate, it's legal but unjust, it's systemic, and pasted on from generation to generation. And at times its self- inflicted, so if I happen, to step on some toes, I can't apologize for something highlighted on the six o'clock news, all over the internet, and is stretched so far out in the aisle, of SOCIETIES ROLE, all I can hope for is that it will be a "heart regulating," an "eye opening," "direction managing" encounter.

BEHOLD, "THE POET'S PERSPECTIVE" ON "SOCIETIES ROLE."

"SOCIAL EVENT"

Young man caught up in "society's role"
Trying to get over but his note seemingly came due
Someone you loved, you liked, and you ran with
Could have been you
Never thought it would happen to him
Because he always tried to stay up on his game
Always tried to stay two or three moves ahead
He wasn't that's why he never saw it coming when it
came...

Dea. Charles E. Peterson Sr. - "The Poet."

SOCIETY'S ROLE, is addressing situations, circumstances, and causes which affect the harmony of today and the built-in factor that carry over into tomorrow. Society's Role relates to, in part, the negative influences and causes that emulate and eradicate the strides made by generations gone by, of a people and a nation. In our Society, there are those who are intentionally profiled and manipulated by its ever present influence.

SOCIETY'S ROLE is a combination of time spans, events, and in many ways, the expected reaction of a given situation, social structure or percentage thereof. It takes us by another's will against our will and strives to deny us, free will.

There have been many unknown soldiers (and known soldiers, some who've marched to the beat of a different drummer), who have won many battles against corruption in our society, yet haven't fallen prey to the inter-struggle and entangling of society's role. We have allowed ourselves to become a nation who would rather incarcerate than educate, who would elevate the right of free speech over prayer, and on more than one occasion allow the will of a few to outweigh the votes of the majority.

Surely, we stand, as a nation of intellect, power and influence, undeniably equal to any threat of war that may come upon us. But it has been said, "If we were to defend our nation the way we fight the war on drugs, we'd soon be speaking a foreign language."

Lastly, a principle worthy of unity or that boast equality for all can't be efficiently effective with so many of its people subjected to "Society's Role," it can only be managed or maintained by adhering to a sound foundation; this one being of the people, for the people and by the people.

"It is easier to build strong children then to repair broken men."

Frederick Douglass

—

"SOCIETY'S ROLE"

SOCIETY'S ROLE

Have you ever questioned (or are you questioning) a decision you made? Because you know it was the one, or one of the ones, that changed life (or could change life) as you know it. And as you found (or fine) yourself "a foot and a half" over the line you recognized (or recognize) it as one of those:

"POOR CHOICES"

Today's choices could affect the rest of your life

Poor decisions can cause hardship and strife

Choices made without consequence evaluations

Are those that becomes tomorrows bad situations

A wise man enters each day with a plan

Down trodden or disappointed maybe but on a plan he stands

Payment usually comes through foresight and preparation

On hope prayer faith and through inspiration

Tomorrow's blank page is the new beginnings the future brings

Problems made today hampers or destroys tomorrows dreams

Think about it, could the consequences of your decision affect your plans? Not just your plans for the present but your future plans. Remember "a fool rushes in, where wise men wouldn't dare to tread." Don't let angry, jealousy; revenge, love, or pride put you a foot and a half over a line that "common sense" and "wisdom" tells you, you dare not go.

"A wise man enters each day with a plan"

Faith is an awesome power to possess, and when you're at hope's end, not that you didn't start from this point, to achieve the desires of your heart. But after all else has fail, you're right here now, "one on one". And if you know like I know there's not too many things more powerful then:

"A MOTHER'S PRAYER"

A child caught up in society's role

Mother home praying for his soul

Out in the world running out of control

To blind to see but the story is yet to be told

How did he make the turn, and prevail

Even he had excepting a fate of going to hell

Reason being is "a mother's prayer"

Spiritually praying for his deliverance and care

Powerful spirits watch and observe

Responding with blessings he did nothing to deserve

A "mother" in constant prayer that he'd repent

Yielding all to "God" so his spirit would be heaven sent

Ever vigilant in praise and prayer

Remembering that "God's judgment" is always "beyond" fair

It took a while to realize the significant of a "praying mother." But looking back and seeing how at times I found myself, let's just say "a foot and a half over the line," and yet somehow, some way. I received "unmerited favor" I can and have thanked "God for:

"A MOTHER'S PRAYER."

Another because that others have sworn by, others lean on, and continue to voice as reason. But it or they are no longer acceptable, because too many others have superseded the beginning and found the avenue of success. Echoing to future generations that, "it's not where you come from, or starts from that defines you." So even if you find yourself behind, coming out the gate, don't allow it to be defined as your,

LET DOWN

Maybe society has let you down

Hemmed you up and

gave you the run around

Your screams well pronounced without a sound

But that's not why you are prison bound

Maybe your "old man" let you down

You had to grow up with him not around

Maybe the world do owe you someway or somehow

But that doesn't seem to matter right now

Because your freedom has been taken away

With it your, right to be effective in what you say

Maybe since you were a child you've got the short straw

Been in and out of trouble with the law

Can't say I've seen or know all the things you've saw

Or how that overall has rubbed you raw

But I know how it's hard growing up - trying to find a place to stand

Feeling like life had dealt me a bad hand

And there are many others who felt their homes were also-ran

Who didn't forfeit their freedom, but vowed to fight on, and formulated a plan

So, there it is, don't allow the past, your present situation, or a cloudy outlook for the future cause you to feel "Let Down," because being "LET down" is often the foundation that causes many of us to "STAND UP." So don't "you" throw in the towel, before you really test the ropes, (for at a young age, you are only in the early rounds) of life.

Don't ever give up for there is reason and purpose for your journey. Though you may often find yourself off stride, if you live only in the moment you'll surely be denied. Find solace in knowing it's not always the destination, but often the completion of the journey, that brings fulfillment.

"PUTTING YOUR DESTINY, IN HARMONY WITH JEOPARDY"

Just for clarity,

If you're living in a fantasy

Your reality, is still your responsibility

And "you're putting "your destiny in Harmony, with, Jeopardy

Like when you're young and get too involved socially

Can ignite your sensitivities

Which could prematurely, arouse your sexuality

This could put your Destiny, in Harmony, with, Jeopardy

Or when you think no one's watching and you see an opportunity

To acquire something illegally

Which once caught will put you before the court of legality

Putting your Destiny in Harmony with Jeopardy

If you're sneaking around playing a pre- arranged role in society

And someone's telling you that this short cuts a guarantee

Ask yourself is it worth your integrity

And would you be, putting your Destiny in Harmony, with, Jeopardy.

So if it's in you to gain the victory, be partly in control of your legacy

Have a life blessed with quality, that will eliminate the jeopardy,

Cause your Destiny, to be in Harmony, with the TRILOGY.

Remember that there are some things we do that have instant ramifications, others that may last for a life time, and may only measure but "a moment in time."

Putting your Destiny, in Harmony, with, Jeopardy...

Where are you going, do you have a goal? What do you want to be when you grow into your own? Have you set your priorities in order? Have you got any targets in sight? If not it's time to:

TAKE AIM

If you evade or avoid your calling

You become blind unto your purpose or cause

Aim or vision is lost or obscured

At some point intention or destination is blurred

Nothing from nothing measure not

You can't add up what you haven't got

Hit that invisible target accidently without aim

Nothing from nothing yet measures out the same

A plan is usually crafted and fashioned from the desire to be, or a vision that at times won't let you be. So, if you are seeing things, you might want to pay a little closer attention, for it might be a good target to "take aim" at.

If You Aim At Nothing You Hit Nothing

It's not always visible, maybe reasoned to be highly unlikely, or no way. But the statistics verify that it's going on right under your nose. Maybe a close friend, or even your best friend. They always have an excuse, reasoning, their upbringing, their "oldman, hard times, the job, jealousy, etc.. But whatever their reasoning, they have become "predators."

And long before the neighbors say, " who could have thunk it," yada, yada, etc.. you knew, suspected, or even witnessed "the predator," attacking:

"THE PREY"

It's a secret

He don't want told

The image he portrays

Could no longer be sold

But with one "black eye" to many

The truth begins to unfold

He's a nice guy, every body's friend

But no one was aware of the beast within

Well, I wouldn't say no one

Because there were those who knew

Someone close to him and someone close to you

Battered beaten, and depressed,

Yet, trying to hold on to the grotesque

For love's sake, the children's sake, pride sake'

She continue to make the same mistake

Defending his actions, taking the blame,

Denying his sickness, barring the shame

Battered women, abusive men,

Silent witnesses, unworthy friends

It's a travesty, I must say

For when he becomes "the predator"

She becomes "THE PREY"

Don't be the one to say, "I wish I had done or said"

Because, that usually comes after a tragedy, or someone's found dead

There's no way around it, "Never mind my bad English. I'm talking about your buddy, your homeboy, your friend. You've been hanging for months, years, a lifetime. He's always tried to cover it up, or reason it out, but we know, (like he knows,) that there is no perfect crime.

Don't be the one to say, "I wish I had done or said," Because, that usually comes after a tragedy, or someone's found dead

WHEN HE COMES CALLING

When the Death Angel comes - Your time is not negotiable

His mission and purpose - Is the collection of Souls

For the mystery of life isn't death - But the usual untimely arrival

Of the administrator for whom the bell tolls - ...

For he comes in all seasons with a quota to fill concerning us all..

Charles E. Peterson Sr. (The Poet)

It doesn't take but a moment to choose to act out of pain, anger, revenge, or even a well thought out plot or scheme. But whenever you think you've got to act or respond in an adverse way, take that moment and use it for:

"CONSEQUENCE EVALUATION"

Don't ever make a move without using common sense
Do what you think is right if you can withstand the weight
Something is always in need of a decision
Permanently, temporarily, immediately, preferably before it's too late
Stupid decisions are often made without consequence evaluation
Because of pride or fear we often sub come, or lose our way
You have to look beyond situation or circumstance
Are responsible for your decisions, actions, and even what you say
Temporarily you may be disillusioned but remember consequence evaluation
Frustrated and angry, but remember this revaluation

"CONSEQUENCE EVALUATION" is taking a moment to evaluate the cost of your intent. A good way to measure the thought is often to measure it with the ruler of "COMMON SENSE."

Don't Do Something Permanently Stupid Because You Are Temporarily Frustrated.

Man I haven't seen you in a "month of Sundays." "Wow", he was so young. You've probably heard one of these or many other such salutations at "going home celebrations". But the ones that stands out the most to me are, you know the ones where it's said "we've got to stop meeting like this," "here we are again," at another:

"SOCIAL EVENT"

Young man caught up in society's role

Trying to get over but his note seemingly came due

Someone you loved, you liked, and you ran with

Could have been you

Never thought it would happen to him

Because he always stayed up on his game

Always tried to stay two or three moves ahead

He wasn't that's why he never saw it coming when it came

Didn't believe that fat meat was greasy

Like the "Ole man" once said

You keep playing with danger

You could wind up DEAD

He lay there someone else breathing in him the breathe of life

It seemingly on a thin line and waning

We know he fought the good fight of survival

But the end results need no explaining

I wish someone had said something that could've changed his perspective of life

Done something to let him know that life overall is worth living

Said something to extend his vision of life beyond a few "blocks in "the hood"

Extend his vision of years beyond the few he thought he'd been given

Because here we go again "meeting and greeting" and burying someone who's died at a very young age - Someone in life you possibly called Brother or Friend, who in life you scarcely visited, but in death his service you can't wait to attend - Yea, here we go again "meeting and greeting" and burying someone who's died at a very young age

Because many funerals have become "social events" with death taking center stage

Because many funerals have become "social events" with death taking center stage

It's happening more and more each week and it gets harder and harder to bare. How can we get you to listen, to stop putting yourselves in harm's way, for pride, for "small change," or for "fifteen minutes of fame," we've all been to one too many, "fatal meeting and greeting" affairs.

I wish someone had said something that could've changed his perspective of life

Whether it's a stick up, a carjacking, snatching a purse, dealing drugs, assault, or b&e, they all come with a basic amount of time to serve for the committed crime. But that's not the biggest risk, for it's what could happen during the crime, when someone may feel justified in using deadly force even for a misdemeanor attempt.

"CRIME DOESN'T PAY"

Don't do it for the sake of getting paid
When you lay your head down you'll be afraid
That during the heist you were made
And you'll also wonder if you'll be betrayed
Don't do it, it's not worth the time you'll have to do
Not if, but when they catch up to you
It's not just a line, there is no perfect crime
And you shouldn't do the crime if you can't do the time
And that's only if nothing goes wrong
But if so this could be your swan song
You could come up against resistance strong
And all your dreams and goals would be gone
So don't let anyone lead you astray
Someone's always trying to find a quick and easier way
You'll get caught and go to prison not jail
Your life will then become a living hell
Going to a system where you become the prey
Another reason you should acknowledge that crime doesn't pay

One of the greatest loses for being convicted of a crime is the loss of your freedoms. Your ability to prosper, vote, your voice, but the greatest lost would be your life.

You'll get caught and go to prison, not jail - Your life will then become a living hell

58

DON'T DO IT, IT'S NOT WORTH THE TIME YOU'LL HAVE TO DO.

If you don't know the "three strike rule" it will be kind of hard for you to understand the total "ramification," of the pre-existing situation. A set in motion "profiling," often unaware, natural occurrence, observed in "all phases "of the legal system. That leaves those, born under the "three strike rule" profiled, young, black, and man:

"PRISON BOUND"

How is it that the vast majority incarcerated, are from one race?

And many because of their color wind up catching "a case"

Why can't we reach and understanding that's well understood

Do not allow the traps of the system and society to bog us down in the hood

Our problems in part is because the tribal mentality has begun to fade

Young and old experience a "gap" because certain fundamentals are disobeyed

Men have lost the will to reason to give the next man the benefit of the doubt

Become programmed or entwined in a system designed with nary a way out

Poor brother caught up in, society's role

Really didn't understand just trying to reach a goal

Introduced to the streets trying that alternate route to succeed

Streets that suck the life out of a man, never fulfilling what he needs

Only thing he could see was trying to find a place to stand

Never realizing that he was but a pawn in a master plan

Beat by a system designed to keep you down

Others before him fail, falling to a system that's world renown

Unusual statistics confirm separate and unequal laws

No one though acknowledges "legal slavery "as the cause

Don't get caught in a system so profound or you'll become prison bound

Our hope is you'll do the math, it's not "trick- a dummy - tre", it's that common sense, math you know, "there's no such thing as a perfect crime" "if you do the crime you do the time," and that age ole favorite "you reap what you sow." So let's work on the "gap" from both ends, because communication is the major key. And I know that, that "trust" issue" will take some work (on both ends), but "if we keep doing the same thing we've (seemingly) always done".... And we all know the completion and meaning of that partial quote.

How And Why Do Our Young Men Become PRISON BOUND.

Issue will take some work (on both ends), but "if we keep doing the same thing we've (seemingly) always done".... And we all know the completion and meaning of that partial quote.

*How And Why Do Our Young Men Become PRISON BOUND.

I'm late, and I apologize. For as sure as "THE URGENCY OF NOW," is now. Now has spanned decades. Now has grown into a system "dedicated to an unknown cause." and by the time our young men realize what it "really" is, and their parents and loved ones get
them to start to listen, they are already "taking a turn" in "the legal curve."

A simple "turn" presumed, but one that have or could turn into that "elongated S-S-S-S-S curve." Because of often separate and unequal laws, and sentencing we face:

"THE URGENCY OF NOW"

The system has long been in place

Having knowledge of it hasn't slowed its pace

Entangled in a system from which it's hard to escape

Usual efforts only get one caught up in the red tape

Response or the lack of, to "The Urgency' we need rearrange

Getting involved gives us the only chance for change

Enslaved minds though find it hard to gather on one accord

Needing to stand as one to oppose the legal discord

Challenging the system from within opposing that which is inhumane

Young boys (and girls) given up on, by the third grade, it's a shame

Ours must "NOW" be the generation to send out the "S.O.S." (Save Our Sons)

Fathers, forefathers, and our leaders have fallen short in their quest

NOW is the time to implement change so our sons won't be "prison bound"

Ours is to move to the beat of the drum that makes that "VITAL SOUND"

With hearts and minds on one accord - we'll strive together for a "Just reward"

I can't put it any clearer the system isn't seemingly, founded on "education but incarceration".

When "the prison system" ranks among big business, school systems are being closed, teachers are being laid off and forced out of their chosen professions. Well let me slow down, I'm just expounding on my right of free speech. Wouldn't want to step on anybody's toes, let alone open up anybody's eyes, or ears (shh) (but, can you hear me now? Legal slavery, separate and unequal laws, people sitting on their hands, "just because you're no longer struggling don't mean the struggle is over." And just because I appear to be whispering, I'm still shouting out "The Urgency Of Now."

But that's the reason I come, "as one crying in the wilderness trying to open the eyes of the children of man before they are harvested by minds of destruction".

"Getting involved gives us the only chance for change"

"There can be no progress without change" I know you've heard it before. But if you find yourself in a position to implement such change, then you should know that it begins with Right now is your opportunity to show mercy, forgiveness, or introduce change by your actions. And charge the recipient(s) with:

"THE DECREE (YOU OWE)"

Stop the violence don't let another young brother fall -- Open up your hearts and ears and hear the call. It's time that we establish a "New Decree" A world wide effort that all men can see. An effort to build on and up - hope and trust -- A decree like "pay it forward" that shall apply to all of us -- A decree like the old proverb That when asked what can be done to repay your reply, **"to bless ten others and charge them the same way"** -- A decree that simply say that in my blessing you, **"You Owe"** - By sparing the seed you allow the culture to once again grow

A Decree that makes us look back, from where we came
Realize the blood running through our veins are the same
A Decree that holds you accountable to the "whole"
One that if you violate shall eat at your very "soul"
A Decree that re- establish the tribal mentality
It takes a whole village to raise a child (especially in today's reality)
You Owe, your fathers and forefathers who paved the way
Those known and unknown soldiers that gave their lives one day
You owe, "God" who said in "His Word" **"thou shall not kill"**
A Decree called "The Ten Commandments" that in part abides still

We now set in motion this awesome seed
Once you become aware of you are convicted to take heed
Unto those who blatantly refuse to honor to "the Tenth Decree"
May your judgment bear swift witness to a "LIVING DECREE."

Let's "do the math." Add (because/so/because of/because of/ because of/you owe)

YOU DID'NT GET THIS FAR ON YOUR OWN

OUR EFFORTS (THAT THEY ARE NOT INVAINE)

UNDESERVING FAVOR SHOWN TO US (FOR YOU)

OTHERS SACRIFICING THEIR ALL FOR THE CHILDREN OF TOMMORROW

WISDOM, KNOWLEDGE, AND UNDERSTANDING ENTRUSTED TO YOU TO PASS ON

EACH OTHER A CHANCE TO GROW UP TO LIVE BEYOND "THE NOW"

= (Y-O-U-O-W-E)

You've seen it, maybe even lived through it, you might have even by reaction to it caused it, and if you are one who's directly responsible for it, know that "it" is like a "parasite" that's been feeding on us for not just "decades" but for "centuries." Why some of the things we do, ways we act and react, some believe, have been intentionally "bred" into us. And is part of:

THE UNSPOKEN PLAN/

There's an evil element among us,

We're playing right into their hands

They're proving we can destroy ourselves better than they can

The works of Martin, Malcolm, and Mandela

Are being pushed aside,

Because there are those among us being led to believe

The worth of a man is measured by a gun

Equal force, materialistic things and pride

You might as well don the white robes and hood, Brother Man,

Because you're doing the work of skin heads, the like, and the

kul klux klan

Gangs killing one another, black on black crime

Evil infiltrating our families, neighborhoods, and minds

Neighbor against Neighbor, Brother against Brother, Fathers against Sons,

Obituaries at an all-time high, neighborhoods being flooded with guns,

Fentanyl, other drugs, alcohol, stuff all meant to keep us off stride

Illiteracy, red lining, segregation, unemployment, People living outside

Divisions in religion, social standards, politics and even color itself

Easily side tracked from the cause, our reality, and destroying ourselves

I said, the hood, is intentionally being flooded with drugs, guns, and alcohol,

We're being bombarded, bamboozled, abased, by our owe hands we fall

Subjected to the rules of "The Unspoken Plan" we do exactly what they expect

Gamely exterminating nationally our culture in deliberate effect!!!

Don't miss it, it's spelled out for you, but you see it every day, it's like that "itch that you can't scratch," the "wound that won't heal," and "the long night that eludes the dawn of a new day." But is it, is it, because "an enslaved mind is rarely freed"?

"THE UNSPOKEN PLAN"

It was possibly the greatest "slight of hands" performance unseen by the
majority of a nation, when "Justice" was replaced with "legality." Oh, it was
"subtle," was something that was meant for the minority, not the majority.
It wasn't a fast ball it was more like a "slloowwww" "knuckleball," with a
diabolical hook know as:

"THE LEGAL CURVE"

I see it, I see it, I see it, and no one seems to give it the magnitude of its magnitude

For it's yet viewed as business as usual, the system, the method, or the legal way

It's the conjuring of imaginings that now makes it legal but not just

It's what causes the chains to bind our hands and mines to except the reality of the day

It's a system that teeters on the edge or verge of corruption

By its deliberate fashioning of separate and unequal laws

By the building of prisons for its children before the founding of schools

By adhering to the rights of man before honoring "God's Word" as a cause

It holds a certain responsibility for the world condition as we know

It holds us all hostages by keeping us subjective by standing on a "legal curve"

As we stand in the need of justice it closes both eyes

As we come to the system seeking what we rightfully deserve

If I think about it for more than a moment it weighs heavy on my heart

If I reflect on all the sacrifices it's easy to realize its monumental cost.

If I factor in "justice" being replaced by "legality," it's easier to understand

The hampering of the benefits we've gained and the damages from all we've lost

All the "legally justified immoralities" and man's inhumanity to man

Has turned our nation in a direction we dare not go

The willingness to judge on a "legal curve"

Has caused its people to "yet" be a divided entity, when it's united we should grow

Many know that the greatest injustice amongst men, is "man's inhumanity to man"
And "justice denied" may have begun with that "slloowwww knuckle ball," but it has
turned into a wicked "Legal Curve."

"Where justice is denied, where poverty is enforced, where ignorance prevails, and where any one class is made to feel that society is an organized conspiracy to oppress, rob, and degrade them, neither persons nor property will be safe."

Frederick Douglass

...“AND THERE I WAS”

I WAS BORN WITH A GOLD LOCK AROUND MY MIND

THE DOCTOR STOLE IT WHEN HE SMACKED MY BEHIND

HOW HE COULD BE SO CRUEL I'M STILL TRYING TO FIND

AND THERE I WAS

I FLEW AROUND THE WORLD RACING A JET

JUST TO WIN A MICKEY MOUSE BET

BUT, IF YOU GAVE ME 5 MILLION DOLLARS WE WOULD

STILL BE IN DEBT

AND THERE I WAS

I RACED A COMET AROUND THE SUN

NOT FOR MONEY, GLORY OR FUN

IT WAS JUST SOMETHING I HADN'T DONE

AND THERE I WAS...

> *Ulysses R. Peterson (Formerly K. A.) “Dezoc” or “The Mad Doctor”*
> *(a “special quote” from my Brother” Doc,” Much Love, WORD”)*

You might think there's nothing worse than someone with an "Attitude" problem. But to me it's someone who'll follow along even when they are aware that they are being pushed, prodded, or taken beyond a point of reason. An often life changing moment, that if you don't speak up with authority, you could find yourself "a foot and a half across the line," excuse me but you need to get an:

"ATTITUDE"

Always try to be aware of those around you

Taking in consideration the direction friends lead

The places they go, people they meet, and the things they do

Inputting your own opinion adding your own perspective

Trusting occasionally in your own point of view

Using your own judgment if you feel that's the way to go

Deciding even if you have to go alone or be one of a few

Each of us often must take a stand even if it means starting anew

Just think about all the life changing moments where everybody involved didn't really know. And now they are paying a price whether small or great. I wonder if things would have turned out different if they had known and shown a little "Attitude."

It will prove to be one of your greatest tests, there's no doubt about it. It often comes down to integrity, morals, courage, and character. It establishes, occasionally whether we will be leaders or followers. An avails us the knowledge that makes us aware that "the loudest voice is rarely the wises"

"THERE COMES A TIME" (GOING AGAINST THE FLOW)

Peer pressure sometimes that's a copout

You've got to be your own self man (or woman)

There comes a time in all of our lives when we've got to take a stand

We can't always flow or go with the flow

Being part of the gang sometimes surely is the way to go

But every now and then your posse, your hommies, your boys (girls),

Group, squad, team, or crew, whatever name given to the inner circle you know

Heads down uncharted, possibly life changing, dangerous waters

And you know in your spirit that you reap that which you sow

And when they wouldn't hear the voice of reason you simply just say "no"

And when you feel in your heart you made the right choice for you

You turn about, even if all alone, stroking against the flow

And as you fill the "current" in your face

There is more often no greater "self -satisfaction" you'll ever know

You're out there often standing up against popular opinion, refuting the norm, and going against the flow. Don't be overwhelmed by the "rush" of the current.

There comes a time in all of our lives when we've got to take a stand

It's a jungle out there, there are predators and there's game, and those who are always trying, to run game.

And there are seeds sown in this jungle that grows and bares fruit that if consumed, or sold, becomes a means to an end.

So beware the young, the unfamiliar, and the naïve, entering the jungle, for you shall reap:

"THAT WHICH YOU SOW"

You can believe what you want to believe
Your reality often hinges on what you perceive
But if it seems too good to be true don't be so naive
For someone is always trying to deceive
Do you know what's my pet peeve ?
When we can see the signs and the truth we won't receive
Leaving family and love ones to suffer because you didn't believe
That which you sow you shall receive
How many before you started out with a mark to achieve
Got caught up in the system now their families grieve
Saw the signs but pride wouldn't let them leave
Thought they were ahead of the game but now we bereave

Let self-destruction be your pet peeve.
When you can see the signs draw the line don't be deceived
Choose not to play the part and your family will be relieved
Because you are aware that, "that which you sow you shall receive"

It's simple, take a minute (a full minute), and take a look at the man (or woman) in the mirror. Where're you going, what are your plans, and are you on course with your dreams or goals, or are you caught up or caught in something, in some way? If so this is as good a time as any, to change directions.

If you for some unknown reason haven't realized that there has grown a great void in the reasoning and understanding of the generations, then know we need your help in the search to find:

"COMMON GROUND"

Wearing the harshest times he's survived as a banner and shield

Standing on a principal of no retreat from his heart it's real

Believing that the absences of fear defines the true character of a man
And that ultimately violence begat violence on that principle he stands

Going toe to toe with wisdom claiming justification through sorrow

But can't add up yesterday and today to formulate a vision of tomorrow
Claiming the pain of this generation is somehow someway the real pain

More pain then my pain, or any pain our forefathers could've sustained
Standing on a principle that runs parallel to fifteen minutes of fame

Without the wisdom to verify the true origin of his pain to claim

Willing to defend to death the right to die against insurmountable odds

Not daring to live facing those odds believing his wisdom's beyond Gods
Can't see the past's significance and how it relates to the reality of today

Not giving respect or credit to those who sacrificed, and made the way

Willing in some ways unknowing to except his plight as his cross to bear

Screaming a silent scream caught in society's role that justice isn't fair

Yet boldly facing his fathers, and all the demons of his forefathers

But instead of fighting for the cause you'd sacrifice to become martyrs
But in the midst of calamity they found a "common ground" to stand
To unite as a people live for a cause worthy of dying for the good of man

They too went forward "often in chains" facing insurmountable odds

But they (as we) learned not to rely on our will or strength but on Gods

They've lived their lives and history has documented their efforts made

But you're yet to make your mark as you travel on the road we laid

They built on a Solid Rock your generation often builds on shifting sand

They planted plotted and schemed to survive you're yet to reveal a plan

They encouraged us to be wise beyond our years we now encourage you

Yet seeking that "Common Ground" that'll help to bring you through

If this doesn't apply to you, then don't take it to heart, I'm reaching out to those that it does, because of the issues that has always been, that more often prevents us from securing "Common Ground."

I don't get it, it used to be respect was a given, at least until there was cause, and family may have had its share of infighting, but they stood toe to toe against outside interference. And we were not only mindful of our past, but in tune with it.

I AM (WE ARE) LOST

Why do I do the things that I do

Why do I show disrespect?

Why do I disrespect my elders, my family, my God?

Is that which I give that which I should expect?

I am lost, a shadow of a being

Nothing like our ancestors envisioned me or us to be

I am lost because only through my eyes am I seeing

Distorting a cycle, that blinds my or our spirits reality

Who do you think you are?

And what truth will you heed

How many doors were pried open for you

So you'd have the opportunity to succeed

I am lost, for I cannot see how

Many of the good seeds have come up as weeds

In a ground tilled in blood, sweat, and tears

By the sacrifices from those whom, the ground yet bleeds

I don't get it, can't rap my mind around the depth of the struggle, and the present outcome, at this point. Where and when did we lose that tribal instinct, and be empowered with that, it's all about me philosophy.

In A Ground Tilled In Blood, Sweat, and Tears

Don't be so quick to judge your effort by who finished the race first, who won the game, or who got the best grade. Did you give it your best effort? Because sometimes we miss the mark because of our lack of preparation, being side tracked, distracted, or our approach was simply wrong for whatever reason. So finishing second, fourth, or last doesn't make you a loser, if you understand that a "Winner" is someone who always "strives" to find something positive in every "worthwhile" effort. Now that's:

"A WINNER"

When the challenges of life confronts

You will surely be tested by its stunts

Give your faith a fighting chance for success

Your effort is what will cause the spirit to bless

Best in the race of life isn't always the one who wins

You're judged by a higher power when this life ends

Always strive though, your best to achieve

A worthy effort in life just as honoring what you believe

Winner isn't always defined -by the first to cross the finish line.

If you ever cross that finish line last, remember that you were still far ahead of all of those who weren't in the race. But remember that the race isn't over until you "evaluate" and learn from the effort.

When You Give Your Best You're Always A Winner

Many times the trials of life can suck the air out of the room, or blind you from your original goals or plans. It's a gradual, unnoticed constant flow, unmeasured by the measure of time. And is often only recognized when you lookback and see that, which you dreamed or envisioned, is or could be a:

"LOST CAUSE"

Have you experienced life as a long haul

You know like with your back up against the wall

Lost over all more than you've gained

Who or what do you blame

You look a little or somewhat off track

Were you by chance planning a big come back

Created this scenario of success

To succeed in your planned quest

Be you aligned with your vision or not

Because many have often given more than they've got

Of rhyme and reason you commit recommit and plod on

Who could have known your sense of direction was gone

You had made a major turn amidst failure, heartache, and pain

Had your vision marred because of what you had to sustain

To achieve it you may have had to forsake your purpose to fulfill

Be lost in the moment, in the now, and maybe, you're lost still

Maybe it was back at that fork in the road, you know where you took the shortcut, the alleged shortcut. Or when you listened to someone whom you knew wasn't even going in your intended direction. Maybe that was where you first questioned:

"HAVE YOU LOST WHO YOU WERE CREATED TO BE BECAUSE OF WHO YOU HAD TO BE"

We are the strength of our generation, a voice speaking to the children of men, through the wisdom of our fathers. We are conveying the need for men to step forward as Fathers, role models, leaders, and men of faith, Men of character, integrity, and moral conscience the sum of the matter needed:

"STRONG MEN"

Weak by the standards of role models needed

Men, young men, blinded by the world system heeded

Wait on others to step up to the plate

For the strong and willing to bare the weight

An obvious flaw in the character of the children of men

Opportunity to train up a child, in the "Way," lost again

Strong though is the faith of those who believe

Men devout, faithful, proclaiming a crown to receive

Make a way, out of no way, for other's worries to relieve

Them as I, bare witness that you be not deceived

Some would say that to bring men up to such a standard or expect them to well "reinvent the wheel" so to say, is an unreal expectation. But as always the seed of "hope" has been planted in the children of men. So with a little more weeding, pruning, and faith we'll be raising "Strong Men" beyond being able to get our "row" out.

Weak Men Wait For An Opportunity Strong Men Make Them

With a lot of our young men and women being exposed and over exposed to all the risqué life styles of the rich and famous (being it stars or jocks), or the hardcore "thug" or "rap" styles with all the "sag" and bling, bling, bling." They seek "role models," so it's up to those of us often, who has their primary care and consideration at hand (whom they seem to rarely listen to at first), to instill in them that it's (more then) the wisdom of the mind, the will of the heart, and/or the skill of the hands, that truly tallies:

"THE TRUE MEASURE OF A MAN"

What is the true measure of a man?

Is it judged by status, wisdom or might Endurance, charisma, or height

By "the old schools" a man's word is his bond

Or by the "strength of the metal" it takes for a father to raise his son

Is it by perception or acclaim based on what others might believe?

By all he accomplishes or all he achieves

Maybe it's about the number of women he has in his life

Or, about being a good and faithful husband to his wife

Maybe It's about being "half the man"; your father was

Yet somehow improving on what he done

Or "twice" the man your father was, being a better role model for your son

What is the true measure of a man?

Is it judged by compassion, charity, or care

Honesty, bravery, or knowing he'll treat you fair

Maybe it's about, what arises in him and how he handles himself when the chips are down

Or how he stepped up when no one else would do it "in a leap and a bound"

Is it about the way he lives his life, or about a moment of sacrifice

What is the true measure of a man?

What he conjures up in his mind - Or what he creates with his hands

Is it about the faith he has in his "God," and how that somehow makes his way clearer?

Or is it overall, all about, how he views the man he "beholds" in the mirror

Now I hope that just about covers it all, but just when you think you've got it all figured out you have to add in the Spirit of the man, what he believes, not what's perceived. The inter man, the man who he is, when he's not trying to be the man we and others think he is, or ought to be.

"What is the true measure of a man, what he conjures up in his mind or what he creates with his hands" ...

Or is it over all, all about, how he views the man he beholds in the mirror.......

Every generation must eventually past the baton of leadership, to the next generation, the hand off, is overall a process that is often viewed as a tug of war. Some believe that we become better leaders when we learn that, "Iron sharpens Iron as one man another." But that's often hard to grasp amidst: "GROWING PAINS"

Can see the path that leads to success

But won't take the first step on the Journey to succeed

Popular enough to be the talk of the town

Yet individual enough to know what to turn down

Old enough to make a baby

But not man enough to raise one

Strong enough to demand to be heard

But not wise enough to listen

Manipulative enough to take the lead

But not courageous enough to follow

Aware enough to see the desperate need

But not adult enough to speak up for change

Yet man enough to be trusted with the future reins

Integrity tested, youth inspected, time sensitive,

Growing Pains

The beauty of the transition most of the time, is when you can release your hold, once they have secured good footing.

"Integrity tested, youth inspected; time sensitive", "Growing Pains"

The ultimate measure of a man is not where he stands in moments of comfort and convenience, but where he stands at times of challenge and controversy.

Rev. Dr. Martin Luther King, Jr.

If you are going on a trip, even if it's a weekend getaway, or an overnighter, you pack what you think you'll need for the trip. If you are driving, you checkout your vehicle, and one of the last things you check is the mirror, but I come to tell you that in life, being that it's a journey, it's one of the first things, if not the first thing you check, because on a vacation getaway you're looking in the mirror, to see what's behind you. But on this journey of life, you look in the mirror to see where you're at now, and going forward do you need to adjust the mirror. To answer the question;

WHO DO YOU THINK YOU ARE

Whom are you emulating?

Who do you think you are?

Where did you get that imagination?

And has it taken you very far?

Have you ever had a talk with the man in the mirror?

Have you ever looked him eye to eye?

Ever dared to question the direction he was leading

Ever really wondered why?

What if you became aware you aren't who you think you are

That the life you're living isn't the life you perceive

That you were given time to find yourself

And all you need to do is believe

What if it became evident that you were living a lie?

Like being offered the red pill or the blue pill

Awaking in an alternate reality not knowing what's real

Now is the time to start questioning the man in the mirror

Harvesting the seeds of wisdom to see if life and reality are the same

Seeking the answers to the questions unknown

Realizing you may not even know your real name

You're young and change is constant

The present reality, is like a pop up storm

For the present is only temporal

A fluctuation of the coming norm

So question the man in the mirror

And see what he has to say

See if he is leading you in the right direction

Or allowing someone, or something else, to lead you astray

It's a difference when you're going with the flow, then when you choice your own path & way. That's when you have to check to see if you've got your game face on.

There's always going to be another avenue to travel even if it means going back to one of those you bypassed on your way. Maybe you've glanced in the mirror wondering if you choice the right direction after going through a fork in the road. And what of that inviting intriguing, "narrow path," that the man in the mirror," spoke so strongly against. That brought you to the first time you questioned, the direction of:

THE MAN IN THE MIRROR

Whom are you emulating?

Who do you think you are?

Where did you get that imagination?

And has it taken you very far

Have you ever had a talk with the man in the mirror?

Ever looked him eye to eye

Ever dared to question the direction he was leading

Ever really wondered why

What if you became aware you aren't who you think you are

That the life you're living isn't the life you perceive

That you were given "time" only to find yourself

And all you need to do to live "eternally" is to believe

What if it became evident that you were actually being deceived?

Like being offered the red pill or the blue pill

Awaking in an alternate reality, and not knowing what's real

Now is the time to start questioning the man in the mirror

Harvesting the seeds of wisdom to see if life and reality are the same

Seeking the answers to the questions unknown

And realize you may not even know your own name

What if you discovered that you're not really living?

But existing in the midst of another's will

Because by allowed the man in the mirror to choose "time over eternity."

Your living isn't really real

And if you continue on this path

Your fate is already sealed.

Have you ever had to lower your voice, because someone eyeing you questioned if they heard you talking to yourself? Maybe it was a conversation that couldn't be postponed, and instead of stopping, with quick thinking, you took out your phone, and pointed to your ear. Whatever it takes to have the conversation, do it, just don't do it while you are driving.

Patience is said to be the key to the optimum fulfillment. In other words taking a minute or two to check out your options, as you hasten on your way, could and most often does save time, energy, and often face. You know like when you react by saying something, or doing something, in haste, you instantly wish you could take back. Because I've learned that patience is a "virtue," and often a "blessing":

"TO THOSE WHO WAIT"

Good is the desire we strive to achieve

Things often get in the way of what we believe

Come what may we yet try to succeed

To secure want and supersede need

Those who are faithful to the cause

Who are willing to seek, yet to obey the laws

Wait knowing the promise is fulfilled by faith

It's like being "proactive instead of reactive," you know, like good chess players, who often see a few moves ahead. And is not surprised by what the intent your move appears to be, because he has already factored it into his plan, because often times he has "patiently influenced" the decision.

Good Things Come To Those Who Wait

NO JUSTICE NO PEACE

Juries have the right to recommend life or death (but)

Unless the system is just it will destroy itself

Some serving time because of the color of their skin

Trusting in a system boasting equality to all men

Incarcerated because of a Prejudicial Clause

Caught up in a system of separate and unequal laws

Everyone's innocent until guilt is found...

Charles E. Peterson S. (The Poet)

THERE'S NO SECRET TO SUCCESS,

IT IS THE RESULT OF

PREPARATION HARD WORK,

AND LEARNING FROM FAILURE...

COLIN POWELL

"SUCCESS"

What "if" you look up one day and realize that through a lot of hard work, time, and sacrifices you are at the pinnacle of your effort of fulfillment of "Life". But although success is "oozing" from what seems, every fiber of your being, with fame and fortune, and men of stature knowing your name. And although you believe you've covered all your bases, dotted all of your, i's and crossed all your t's. But that something, something inside of you is yet unfulfilled, just to come to the realization that you missed it, that one "if," (right where we all are) in the middle of :

"LIFE"

Life is lived between worst and best
Is an effort lived to fulfill a quest
What occurs beyond "legit" and or mistake
Happens often because of the choices we make
While you make plans trying to accomplish what others expect
You're often hampered by situations of morals and effect
Making your dreams and goals harder to believe
Other obstacles make your plans harder to achieve
Plans are good to make but most people don't understand

Oh, by all means keep on making your plans, but make your plans with a better understanding, that old quote will often have the last word. You know the one that says, "The best laid plans of mice and men"…. For, oftentimes we fall short of our dreams and goals, putting all "the merits of success" on completion, but, oftentimes the journey is more rewarding then the fulfillment of the quest. For:

"LIFE IS WHAT HAPPENS WHILE YOU'RE MAKING OTHER PLANS"

94

It's often hard to keep your focus when the door of opportunity closes in your face, again. But you are not bound by sight, and it's your faith that shall insure that:

"THE DOOR IS OPEN"

When it doesn't seem that opportunity will ever knock

One goal after another fails or is blocked

Door to success seems to be farther and farther away

Closes just beyond your reach holding you at bay

I pray that won't detour you from your goal

Hope you're in it for the long haul, and your faith is a stronghold

Another opportunity which may be right before your eyes

Door that leads to success and not compromise

Opens up other avenues that you never realized

For with in your faith lies the seed to success

You must continue to believe and you'll be blessed

So as you strive to get beyond missed opportunities (for whatever the reason) and your fears, "be patient," and remember, that the door of opportunity doesn't always just open and shut, but more often than not it actually, is the revolving door of "Success."

There it is again that faint whisper that's been a constant, that one thing that for whatever reason echoes around, amidst, and beyond the plans and intentions of the day to day. It's worst then an unanswered question, it's unwavering, it's:

"AN IDEA"

Remember as you strive to be

Nothing is always what it seems

Is this a new beginning?

As the fulfillment of a dream

Powerful are good intentions

As also the thought to succeed

An awakening of a vision

Idea vet that you must heed

Whose responsibility is its maturity?

Time after time it has risen and wouldn't subside

Has been found in visions and dreams

Come before you now and won't be denied

If you are not seeing it altogether, write it down, speak it out, or if you are, and it's legal and original, and you're just not acting on it. Remember, there is no greater change of life, than the birth, of a new idea.

REMEMBER NOTHING IS AS POWERFUL AS AN IDEA, WHOSE TIME HAS COME

96

You're already there ahead of the game, someone whom others seek out for answers; turn to in the midst of the storm, self-reliant, maybe you haven't yet achieved all of your goals, but you have already, maybe unbeknownst achieved:

"SUCCESS"

You shall super cede the norm

Are not afraid of success, a rider on the storm

A trend setter, a mind changer, a leader amongst men

Success is but a destination that's right around the bend

Going over the mountain of your intent

Somewhere where destiny and time are relevant

To an envisioned destination that runs parallel

Eventually overcoming, all obstacles to prevail (to)

Succeed equates destiny, success is now reality

The best way to be successful is not to seek it for tomorrow, but to live it day to day, and to claim it as though it was already tomorrow, living it in the now.

You Are A Success Going Somewhere To Eventually Succeed.

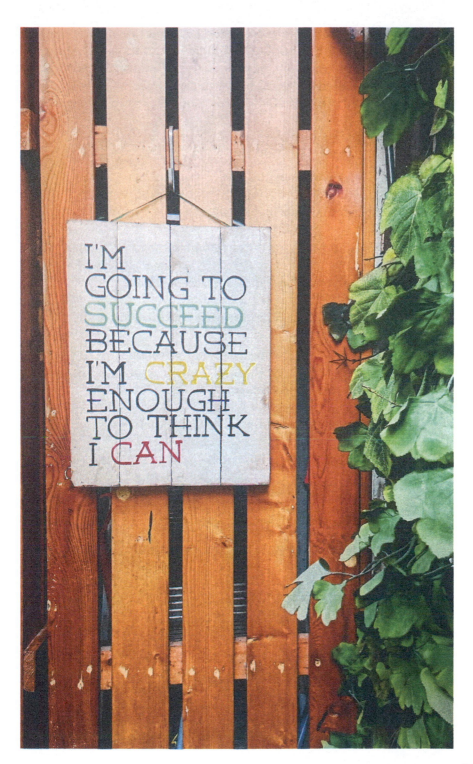

With the fulfillment of the dream, vision, or plans one must intensify efforts to maintain the reasoning and judgment that played a part in your success, or a measure, of your success. Simply said is, "it's a whole lot harder often to operate the vehicle of success, then it is to succeed." To maintain that success you "must" learn to manage:

"WISDOM, POWER & RESPONSIBILITY"

With the grasping of wisdom and understanding

Great is the urge for success and to succeed

Power is now within reach for those who hold the keys

Comes to all in different ways and at different times

Great is the challenge to harvest the power of the mind

Responsibility, if grasped, creates wisdom by design

And is able to conquer the doubts and fears that intertwine

The power and responsibility often engulfs and defines

Ability to distinguish between the two helps us to maintain control

To be able to "manage and regulate" such power with responsibility is the goal

Achieve greatness, help the unfortunate, walk humbly, gain respect, and notoriety

Wisdom is **Power and** with power comes **Responsibility**

There is no limit to success, but there are obstacles that become stumbling blocks. So to harness the power, manage the responsibility, (and maintain it) will take wisdom.

To be able to manage and regulate such power with responsibility is the goal

100

You can't quit now, you've put in too many rounds, to throw in the towel. You've put in the work, been on the ropes a few times, but that was like "rope a dope." You still have a shuffle or two left in you, and you're only one quick flurry away from a T.K.O.. Your strategy's sound and patience an opportunity could align in the next round. It's been a long "bout" but soon you'll be known as:

"AND OVER NIGHT SUCCESS"

It may seem peculiar but in part you have a plan

Often others will abandon you and won't understand

Takes more at times then you have to give

Many times you've had to set it aside to live

Years have been riddled with short comings and strive

Of which it played a part in your day to day life

Sacrifice was made to preserve its quality

To be prepared for such an opportunity

Be in line with and beyond the natural flow

And to help guide your steps as you go

Over and over you commit, recommit, and rehearse

Night after night you nurse your thirst

Success arrives before you know you're in its midst to prove it's so.

"Fools rush in where wise men dare not go." So remember your "fight plan," keep your "guards up" (against procrastination), "focus" (on succeeding beyond expectation), and "dance" (away from doubt and impatience).

**It Often Takes Many Years Of Sacrifice To Be And
Over Night Success**

What is your dream or ambition? Someone once told me that one of the worst things you could ever do is succeed. Because most people drive so hard to get there, but don't realize once they succeed, they'll actually have to "switch" vehicles. To ultimately come to realize they can't handle or operate:

"THE VEHICAL OF SUCCESS"

For as far back as I can remember

Many battles have been lost and won

Times bring about many changes though

We gain much insight but the war wages on

Gain often the advantage with our desire to succeed

The drive the effort beyond our dreams we exceed

Victory seems to be within our grasp onward we lead

But sometimes what we want isn't always what we need

Can't understand why victory isn't "o so sweet"

Operate in a realm where success seems to be sprinkled with defeat

The sweet savor of victory quickly begins to lose its flavor

Vehicle which brought you through the storm begins to labor

Of all the challenges it took to succeed

Success now becomes the new challenge you must heed.

102

Point blank, getting there is only half the battle, "SUCCESS" is a whole "nother" gear "overdrive". Dream bigger, increase or expand your vision, as you drive to get to the "pivot point" of your intent, and by all means," "START ACTING SUCCESSFUL."

"For Many Times We Gain The Victory, But Can't Operate The Vehicle Of Success."

Most everybody is standing up for something now a days you know, cause, cause, cause, or just because. In striving to find ourselves, our reason for being, our purpose we often attach ourselves to existing efforts. Or we stumble on a purpose worthy of our time, energy, and dedication seeking to make a difference, hopefully for the good of mankind. And hopefully you don't just follow the crowd at least do some research, because there is already too many people out here "chasing after an unknown cause." So I ask you:

"ON WHAT WILL YOU STAND"

On what will you stand - And what is your cause
Have you found a purpose - To help eradicate any of society's flaws
For what will you work - And for what will you strive
To whom do you owe homage for being alive
For what would you dare to step out on "thin ice"
Without hesitation without thinking twice
Or rush fearlessly into a burning hell
For your purpose to live for your cause to prevail
Have you found anything worth risking your life
Your "God, "your children, your husband, your wife
Your parents, your people, your vision, your dream,
Have you found a cause worth risking everything
Maybe it's your principles, the truth, your honor, your name,
Your rights, your faith, success or fame
For what "cause" or purpose would you help the children of man?
On your morals and integrity dare to stand
What do you believe in to the greatest degree?
That when others look at you it's in part what they see

Don't sell yourself cheap, putting all your eggs in one basket, because there are many causes that could use your support. I found the secret to committing to a cause is to first, get to know yourself, your values, principles, opinions, character, integrity, you know all the things others are going to see in you.

"For what "cause" or purpose would you help the children of man, on your morals and integrity dare to stand"?

104

You can see it almost as clear as day; you've pieced a lot of it together already. But that "almost" part, has you hesitant or halted, it's what's hindering your progress. The whole vision is like looking at and being served a "whooole elephant." With such an enormous task before you, the first question that comes to mind (as you secure your napkin) isn't, whether it's "medium well or well done." But a question you thought you'd never ask. "How do you eat, an

"ELEPHANT?"

First you ask for a "to go container," containers, then you plan to eat it for breakfast, lunch, brunch, dinner, late night snacks, etc. But it begins, "one bite at a time," just be sure to:

"REMEMBER"

Remember to remember when in search of your quest

That each day in time is but another test

The avenues filled with mounting anticipation

Journey filled with great expectation

Of joy, of need, of wonder, and intrigue

A desire to accomplish, establishes, and succeed

Thousands of thousands begin this daily trek

Miles and miles of not knowing what to expect

Begins oft with a vision or a dream

With high hopes, ambition and great esteem

A leap of faith that parallels opportunity

Single objective to reach your destiny

Step to it than so that the dream or vision is kept

Remember to take one step at a time, until you get your rhythm, balance, or flow, And while you're easing into your vision, picturing the elephant, remember you don't have to eat it all the same way, you can bake it, broil it, roast it, fry it, stew it, put it on a piece of bread and toast it, but before you see yourself all fat and full, just "REMEMBER" to:

Remember That The Journey Of A Thousand Miles Begins With A Single Step.

How often have you believed that you were just one step from reaching your mark, or you needed only one piece to connect a major piece of a puzzle, but there is no better known satisfaction then when you can say,

I HOLD THE KEY

I believe the key to Success is to dare to Try

How can someone else be successful and not I

Only because they took the initiative to Try

Let your dreams and ideas be set free from your mind

Dare to try and success you could fine

There will be those who will tell you dreams don't come true

How can you justify listening to someone with no vision

Easiest way to make what they say be true, is not to try, not to pursue

Keep this poem close at hand, because you know exactly what its saying

Every day it'll dare you to pursue and focus on your plans

"You" now hold the key, to your success, go with God, and be blessed

Trying is not only the antidote against failure it's also one of the major seeds for success.

So, if you want to be one of the few, a key holder, keep trying.

There are many avenues to failure and success, failure often arrives after you've done your best. Sometimes, it's not because of what you've done; you "just" stumble upon success. But if you're in any way like me, giving up is not an option. And you'll find a thin line in line with, Let me be found;

"TRYING"

Let fate cause me to be denied

Time me and see if I've lost my stride

Be this, be that, be the "The True Measure Of A Man"

My Success is found in doing the best that I can

Witness my journey in "TRYING" to "succeed" in what I believe

Don't ever give up for there is reason and purpose for your journey. Though you may often find yourself off stride, if you live only in the moment you'll surely be denied. Find solace in knowing it's not always the destination, but often the completion of the journey, that brings fulfillment.

The plan is or was to, huh, you didn't have a plan. Ok, ok, it's not too late. There's no time to waste it's time to start packing for:

THE UNKNOWN COUNTRY

Plan to become, acquire, achieve, and own

For it is wise to prepare for the coming unknown

Retirement from that which has become life long

But know that although you've planned, things can still go wrong

Live with the understanding that nothing comes with a guarantee

As we all make plans for what we hope we'll see

Though we often must make sacrifices, before it comes to be

There's always staying the course that's the key

No true journey is begun without a plan

Tomorrow is the unknown country, and it's now at hand

Wow, "time is passing like gas," and what you've put off, set aside for, or just under estimated, arrives for some with the rising sun. I wouldn't try to encourage you to invest totally in the "Unknown Country," but to:

"PLAN FOR RETIREMENT, BUT LIVE AS THOUGH THERE'S NO TOMORROW"

"WONDER AND WHY"

Beyond the realm of understanding

Lost in the vast darkness of question

There lies "wonder and why"

Spanning the outer limits of the unknown

Trying to comprehend the unimaginable

Wrestling with reason trying to understand why

Why, why, why, why,..

Dea. Charles E. Peterson Sr.

"ISSUES"

"THE CYCLE" *(ABUNDANCE)*

Looking back to another time and place, I remember a little child, who was asked the question, what is your mother's name? He looked up with the most sincere and affectionate smile and said:

"MOMMA"

*There are many who have answered to that worthy name
Are and have strived to achieve their worthy goals
Many words, that stands alone in their significance
Like many people in their contributions and roles
You are the "e-pit-o-me" of the twain
But our love "eclipses" and runs deeper in our souls
You are that "pendulum," that endured your test of time
Stand or fall, with or without, you endured it all
Alone, at times yet your mountain you continue to climb
Many times you didn't get the recognition you were due
Other times it may've seemed we took the reins and went on
Maybe you had the feeling that we didn't "appreciate you
Momma there is, nor ever was anyone we appreciated more
All your children with all our "love" forevermore*

No matter where life leads you always remember "you only get one "ole girl." So give her a call, a little more often or better yet drop in on her "just because."

"Many times you didn't get the recognition you were due"
("MOMMA")

It's a celebration of life, love, and commitment, an effort to maintain
a level of commitment to be prepared for what if, fueled by a Love that
endures the test of time, and a life that's celebrated in smiles and tears,
baby steps and leaps and bounds, all that culminated in your reflection:

"WHEN YOU LOOK BACK" (MOMMA)

What did it take to manage the years?
To bring your family through
How many times have things gone wrong,
With everyone putting their hopes in you
And how many times have you denied yourself
Because that's what Mothers do
And how many times has twenty-four hours
Not been enough time in a day
To finish or begin what needed to be done
To lead, steer, or support a child along the way
How often have you had to be doctor, teacher, and chef?
To stretch that all mighty dollar when there wasn't much left
How many times have life thrown you a curve
In the midst of thinking that everything was ok
And how many times have you done the wrong thing
In trying to find your way
And how many times has "God" blessed you
When you didn't think you deserved to be
And how many times has "He" made a way
Out of a way that you couldn't see
And how many times have you blessed others, with your gift
In the volume of a song
And how many times has "He" brought you over the highways and by ways
Safely back home
And how many times have you been thanked, for all that you have done
By those who Love and Care the most, your Daughters and your Sons
So *"When You Look Back MOMMA,"* on all you've went thru, and where
it all begun Know there are many Family members and Friends, that Love,
and appreciate "You," for the race that you have run.

Isn't it funny how "thank you" and "I or we appreciate you", sometimes
don't measure up to a lifelong commitment, but how they are often received
as over payment, because, you felt, you had already been paid in full.

114

We've all heard the one about if you tell a lie, sooner or later you'll have to tell another, to collaborate, your story. And if you continue with it, it could become like *"connect the dots,"* which usually brings you to the point where you *"contradict"* the first lie. I have a brother who says, *"if you're going to lie, tell the true."* For a lie is but:

"A CIRCLE INCOMPLETE"

"Oh" to be caught in the dreadful lie

What a shameful way to support an alibi

A lie is but a circle incomplete

Wicket becomes the benefactor of such deceit

Web of deception is what we begin

We tell a lie we'll have to tell it again

Weave that web if you choose

When it comes full circle you're bound to loose

We may at times think it puts us ahead of the game

Try to justify it, or let someone else take the blame

To whatever gain or profit that unduly comes your way

Deceive one or a few it'll catch up to you someday

Deception is and always has been *"a bad road to travel."* Because no matter if it fulfilled *"the short cut of your intent,"* you're destined to take, *"the long way around,"* or wind up on *"the roundabout"*

"Oh What A Wicked Webb We Weave When We Try To Deceive."

Sometimes our pride gets in the way of doing the right thing, especially in the spur of the moment. To look back over the years and remember the many times it took me too long, to muster up that first step, to do the right thing. To not let the issue whether large or small cause a division that could be bridged by simply, and sincerely saying:

I APOLOGIZE.

Most people find it hard to say, "I Apologize"
What I done was not ok I recognize
I made a mistake in judgement my friend
Forgive me I'll try to not let it happen again
Or I recognize, and I apologize
I should have took more time to rationalize
Before I openly criticized
Sometimes it comes too late once we apologize
To offer a hasty avenue of compromise
So before you speak out you might want to visualize
YOU being the one who's being criticized
So you might want to sympathize
Before you choose to criticize, and have to apologize

I know I'm not the only one who had to back track and clear the air. You might have had to do it occasionally, and you may need to do it now. Because it's one of those things that if you don't do it, it won't get done. And it's like a bad smell; it only gets worse with time.

Don't act like you're "The Lone Ranger," because "every day is another test of time." And sometimes no matter how much of ourselves, time, wisdom, money or prayer we put into an effort we still need a "miracle." For often times when we are at our wits end, we find ourselves in the midst of:

"WONDER AND WHY"

Beyond the realm of understanding

Lost in the vast darkness of question

There lies "wonder and why"

Spanning the outer limits of the unknown

Trying to comprehend the unimaginable

Wrestling with reason trying to understand why

Why, why, why, why,...

Sinking, spiraling, gasping, grasping, down to the depths of wonder

Eyes searching, ears perking, nerves twitching, gut wrenching,

Looking, seeking, searching, questioning mind wondering

Wondering, wondering, wondering, wondering,..............

Beyond logic and emotion

Engaged in seeming happenstance, and impromptu

Heart aching quaking, breaking, sadly mistaking

Moaning, groaning, visually cloning, mentally honing, verbally stoning

Up and down to and fro, over and over and over again

Standing boldly on the principle of the thing

The thing that used to be, that was, but is no more

The thing that runs parallel to its own reality

Why, why, why. why........

Blending fading, climbing, reaching for seemingly the unachievable

The afore perceived bird in the hand

The sure thing the answer to the question unknown

The key to the thing

The thing that became counterproductive and ran counter clockwise

The thing that was the right thing, the best thing, the good thing

The thing that became entwined in the often un-breach-able cycle of time

The thing that was the plan, the vision, the thing that was the dream

The thing that has become faint, a glimmer, that which is but a gleam

The thing that runs into "fate and reality" and beyond the efforts of

"try" And leads you to....... "Wonder and Why".......

I don't know about you but I'm not one of those people who passed life's entire test. But I've come to realize that, "time is just a marker, marking the decisions of the mind." So when you find yourself in between "Wonder And Why," (concerning a just cause) and you've planted, watered, and labored. Make a committed decision to pray on it, and let go, and let "God."

"Beyond the realm of understanding"
Lost in the vast darkness of question

118

You rarely ever see it coming, often only recognize it, after you experience a series of slips, mishaps, obstacles, and strains come in tandem. That's when you realize you're in:

"THE SEASON OF PAIN"

When things happen that we can't explain
Like when the "death angel" comes and can't be restrained
When all the reasons seem to be insane
You are going through the season of pain

When there's a mighty effort made to just maintain
When your best yet seems to go against the grain
Like going down the road in the wrong lane
You could be going through the season of pain

When the forecast says sunshine and you're standing in the rain
When you're all dressed up and everyone else is plain
When life seems to repeat itself and livings in vain
You could be going through the season of pain

When you lived through your past but a remnant remain
When your life feels like someone else is holding the reins
When you've been down this road of lost and gain
You've come to realize you're able to endure

"The Season Of Pain"

It's often as constant as the change of seasons, as the rising sun, or the changing weather in Michigan. You know in a certain season how it's said if you are not in a storm, you're coming out of a storm, or a storm is brewing, such is "the season of pain."

119

You can't or won't acknowledge the issue, and therein lays the problem. You are often forward, and opinionated, but won't address your:

"ISSUES"

You build up walls

Have established a guarded point of view

Issues concerning this, issues concerning that

Seeing things differently is natural for you

Saying often what first comes to mind

Using lopsided logic, instead of common sense

Exaggerating your perspective to justify

Serving only long enough to find reason to build another fence

We all have them, and it would be wise to step out of the circle, every now and then to just see if you can tighten up a few "Issues" of your own.

Although we are in many ways still experiencing the after-shock of "911," like "ripples" echoing from shore to shore. And although retaliation came swift and strong, the fire smoldered but hasn't gone out. And that's why our "heightened sense of awareness" leaves us with a bitter taste for:

"THE FLAVOR OF THE DAY"

With war and destruction highlighting the six o'clock news

Those in charge spouting revenge and lighting a very short fuse

An alarming situation a terrible smoking gun

But someone must pay for what has been done

Terror is ever present it's certainly time to pray

For terrorism is the unfortunate "flavor of the day"

War on the home front what have they done

Somebody anybody everybody, call and (remember) 911

The near unimaginable has finally come to be

The thing only thought of in fiction has become reality

Our mighty shores couldn't protect from an enemy within

From another horrid effort of man's inhumanity to men

From a war never declared a cowardly act

Many victims and heroes die because of a sneak attack

There are no rules of engagement civilians are targets as well

The unexpected horror of the reality of a living hell

Many are suspected and suspicions run high

The enemy is often invisible to the naked eye

There's a heighten sense of awareness

The war of the world has finale struck home

We've deployed men our retaliation is strong

We took the war to the terrorist

Even though they died in the effort they made

Those that harbored and protected them are the ones that paid

They destroyed the towers but we towered over them

They awoke "the sleeping Giant" now they're out on a limb

Because the only thing he likes more than "peace and tranquility"

Is proving at the "art of war" he holds "a superiority"

I know, I know, I know that this is a very sensitive issue an there are those who haven't gotten over it and may never get over it. But, when do we interject that violence "begets" violence, and hate "begets" hate, and "if we keep doing the same thing..." and how about the healing process, and the effort it takes to close an open wound. And to not have others suffer or experience the same hurt or demise. I know to some there will never be a right time, but I guess if we can't work it out or won't forgive each other as fellow human beings, Then keep an eye to the sky (in more ways than one)....

"Somebody, anybody, everybody, call and (remember) 911"

We see it everyday somebody on the outside looking in, someone without any place to call home, for whatever reason. Often we tend to judge, criticize, or ostracize them, all within a single glance. Without even considering walking a mile in another man's shoes:

"THE INVISIBLE" (The Homeless)

The invisible band that's spreading across the land

Echo's the humdrum of man's inhumanity to man

The invisible strand has infested - and is out of hand

They are us- be not mistaken and try to understand

Although they have become the "have - not" band

The same way they missed their goals and dreams we can

Many use to be middle class worked many years with a plan

But downsizing, Outsourcing, plant closings, helped create the strand

Who, watched their dreams and goals fade, like sifted sand.

Statistics climb because of the decreases that created the new clan

Many have been lost because of society's inhumane ban

Don't wait until your situation change before you take a stand

Everybody's got a story about how they got here from there, half of them that (for whatever reason,) came up short of their plans. And fell in that great void of life where dreams, goals, and visions go awry. Where to tell you their story, somewhere in the midst of them, I know you'd see how easily misfortune could have "beset" you, because "Life is what happens while you're making other plans". "Often we tend to judge, criticize, or ostracize them, all within a single glance." "But the same way they missed their goals and dreams we can"

They powered a revolution of the mind, an awakening of an awareness that was needed at the time. They noted the main distractions that made many blind, to a reality that they "poetically" defined. Their message was clearly profound, and ahead of their time.

"ODE TO "T.L.P."

Their messages were direct and clear

Hearing their recitations was often severe

Each with their own unique style

Learned artist spouting awareness, truth, and denial

Attacking truth in the raw

Standing on a principle often challenging the letter of the law

Talking about the revolution, fear and otherwise

Promoting the fact that it won't be televised

Outside the circle of the norm

Echoing to the generations "to come," to not just conform

To question, challenge, and remember history

So they'll understand that "freedom" really isn't free

They stood up in an age where equality and segregation were openly at odds, and used their gifts as a "two edged sword" to bluntly and poetically, open up the minds and to help stimulate the cause of our people. Their message is "yet" relevant today. For those who don't know them, look them up for they are:

"THE LAST POETS"

Some are rewarded for doing what comes natural to them, if they see another "brother in arms," in need they do the best they can to help him up. And through humility, they don't expect to be considered a:

"Hero"

They called him a hero

Said he'd made the grade

When he got home he'd have a parade

But he flat out refused their promise

Said all the heroes were in their graves

They said that his actions were

Above and beyond the call of duty

He said all he was trying to do was survive

To get back home alive

They said he'd receive the Bronze Star

And the Purple Heart

He said all he'd done was his part

They said he fought for a cause

Other men were willing to die for

He said that didn't make him a hero

That made him a survivor...

They said the cause out weighted the "opinion"

He said he wasn't there for the cause

He was there "Just Because."

Often many of those who risk it all, is said to have "went above and beyond the call of duty," or gave their lives, for another "brother in arms." Many "were often considered less than those whom they saved". And were only accepted as "a Brother in arms" after they risked it all or "posthumously." For most true, "Heroes are made of those who are often considered, "lesser men."

Have you ever questioned or wondered why or why not, concerning something you really wanted to be or do? Maybe it was something that was seemingly impossible, like being a "Billionaire", or even "flying like a bird." But sometimes we don't always think it through, say for instance like:

TO FLY

As a child I questioned why

Like the birds I couldn't fly

Many fantasies and day dreams now gone by

I'll hop a plane and give it a try

Although I won't be in complete control

I'll yet lift my spirit and my soul

And sour high above the clouds

Country roads and city crowds

And from superman's vantage point

I'll see,cities in their entirety

And sour like an eagle high above

Places I've only dreamed of

Some say that they would fly

The whole world around

If throughout their flight

They could keep one foot on the ground

Flying for the first time is an adrenaline rush, or it could cause an anxiety attack, that could leave some wanting to do it again if they could somehow keep one foot on the ground.

"THE CYCLE"- (ABUNDANCE)

Sometimes abundance is not measured by the fruit which is harvested, but often by the "Power" within the seed. So many of our Forefathers didn't seem to have an abundance of material things to pass on to us, but what they could and did pass on was and abundance of "hope, will, endurance, a sense of Family, and for most of us, the understanding of "Faith." And also, the understanding that we are "overcomers," a people that sacrifice, share, and survive. So what they sowed we reaped, and what we sow, our children shall reap. So it

behooves us "to train up a child in the way that they should go," informing them about the "Cycles Of Life" So they'll be more informed about the debt they owe to the past and future society. And as we pass down "the wisdom of the ages," the "Abundance" is reaped through the "Cycles Of Life" So our children, and children's, children's, children, and the generation to come, shall honor the "Cycles" that link our Forefather's, us, and our seed, and the seeds of our seed together, through past present, and future generations. So as you prepare to leave a "legacy" for the next generation, don't focus so much on the material, but be sure that they are "Well-Schooled," on the

"CYCLES OF LIFE"

128

"PERSONAL"

I can't tell you why it became or ended the way it did, life is filled with twist and turns, opinions and choices. And like everyone else, I've made some good ones and some bad ones.
And I can't tell you why someone else done what they did. All I can tell you is:

WHY I DONE WHAT I DID

I can't tell you how or why I was molded in the miry clay

Know this though unbeknownst to me it lit my path and way

What brought me to a new awareness wasn't totally unforeseen

I knew that I must take this path for I'd seen it in a dream

Done were the days of my youth at a very young age

And what loomed heavily before me was all on another page

Why I had to assume the role of man coming out the gate

I looked within myself for answers, but it was just my fate

Done what needed to be done as I had learned in my youth

What a revelation it was to find a foundation in Spirit and truth

I found myself in the midst of confusion a shadow of a man

Did what needed to be done and now on the Solid Rock I stand

Why me? Oh, I asked the question often during the span of time, as I grew. But learned that there's always a price to pay, even if you do what you believe to be the right thing. But in time, I asked, "why not me"? And as I found another path to travel, "life echoed" "it's not where you start from that defines you."

"I KNOW WHAT I DONE AND WHY I DONE WHAT I DID."

130

It's not always about getting to the top of the mountain, winning, or going places where everybody knows your name. It's often about maintaining the day to day, not striving but surviving, and "believing you shall" endure the challenge:

"ONE DAY"

I always knew that one day we'd prevail

And I know everybody has a story to tell

But I always thought that we'd succeed

Be able to afford more than just what we need - One day

I truly believe that hard work and sacrifice

Is worth more than a roll of the dice

That the work you do will eventually speak for you

And that a sincere effort will be rewarded too - One day

I have always thought that success was but

A line or phrase away, and surely achievable someday

Even when those without dreams or visions couldn't see

I always knew that it would be - One day

And although others have already made their mark

And I at times seem to be stuck on start

You need to know that I already found success - One day

When someone was "moved" by something I wrote and, they read

Or when "in the midst" of my recital by something "the Spirit" gave and I said

For it was and is "His" blessing that got me here

So "one day" when it's all said and done

And my last message has been spun

And my steps has slowed in this race we run

I believe "He'll" finish what "He" begun - "ONE DAY"

There it is again: "It's not about the amount of time you're given but about what you do with the time you're gave." And even though you put in the work, always remember that it wasn't all about "what you conjured up in your mind, or what you created with your hands." But overall "how and why," "He", blessed you to do so, and if you used the gifts in "faith and as a blessing to others.

"That the work you do will eventually speak for you

And that a sincere effort will be rewarded too" - "One day"

132

Can you look back, back unto a time when you couldn't answer how, didn't understand why, and couldn't but question where to go from here? Been there done that, and all though you can't see it, you really couldn't imagine;

"WHAT I'VE BEEN THROUGH"

Thank God we made it

God will bring you through

I can personally testify to it

Don't give up on 'Him" for He won't give up on you

Look to the hills, from which comes your help

Like it or not the load you must bare

What so ever your situation or circumstance

I've come to testify, "He'll be there

Been through the fire, up the rough side of the mountain as well

Through many storms of life but by faith I was able to prevail

You might wonder or be questioning how to survive the "now," or even worse how to at least get back to go, where you had plans and dreams, that now seem to be far out of reach. But I'd like to encourage you to **"REMEMBER,"** what it takes to become **"AN OVER NIGHT SUCCESS."** And often all you need is **"AN IDEA,"** the will to keep **"TRYING,"** and to answer the question, **"ON WHAT WILL YOU STAND"**?

Have you ever been on a job and got caught up in the magnitude of its magnitude, finding that it was always that something, something that needed to be done or hadn't been done. Sure you have, it's called "life."

Chr. "IF I SHOULD DIE BEFORE I WAKE"

If I should die before I wake

And you are still here on the other side

And if I've come up short in what I was assigned to do

Let them know it wasn't because I hadn't tried.

If in my effort those things that I done

Didn't turn out the way I hoped they would

I ask your forgiveness of the man

Whose only intentions was to do the best he could

So if I should die before I wake /And is unable to clarify and set it straight

All those things that went awry

Do tell them as a child of God all I could do was try

So if you saw me going "to and fro"

Often seeming full of wonder and doubt

Don't feel sorry for what you seen me go through

For it took all of that which beset me to get my row out

So if I should die before I wake

And fall short of my dreams, desires, and a measure of fame

Know that once I found myself in the Lord

I found all I needed, and succeeded, in Jesus Name

We all know that "the shortest distance between two points is a straight line" but in life many of us have to take the long way around, you know, like "a long row to hoe."

It's not as though I've ever seen it, or can say that I've even heard it, but I know for sure that I have felt its presence. And it doesn't just observe, it whispers through my spirit. And I'm able to behold:

"THE SILENCE"

The Silence and I have intertwined

Thou many times I may appear to be alone

I've always had the Silence

Even at times when I was within a crowd facing the unknown

Or in the midst of confusion or chaos

I could always turn to the Silence

I noticed as I went to and fro trying

To manage my often heavy load

That there was a "presence" that seemed to

Observe my effort, achieve or fail, I was always

Aware of the Silence

So it was the Silence that I sought

When I couldn't find the answer

When my best wasn't good enough

When I didn't believe that I measured up

When I felt I should be leading, but was behind

It was the Silence, that echoed, I think you can

You can do it, one day at a time, why not you,

The "ole man" bared his weight, the "ole girl" as well

As a child, I often beheld their efforts, determination,

And resilience, and it was there, beyond their weight,

For it was in them, that I first observed, and was embraced by:

"THE SILENCE"

Have you felt it, if so I know you probably haven't mentioned it to anybody? And I know you can't always feel it, but have you found yourself looking around because you "sensed" a "presence."

135

What is. "the true measure of a man," what he conjures up in his mind or what he creates with his hands? It's both, and all of his failures and intends. For with every contact you make you plant a different seed or paint a different picture, or create a different perspective of your;

"LEGACY"

If I were to assess my efforts and intents

Add up and poll my accomplishments

If I could sum up all I said and tried to say

I'd first thank "The Lord" in a special way

For "He" is the Potter" and I'm but the clay

For anything noteworthy, "He" gave me to say

For my main purpose was to lift "His" name in praise

And share what "He" blessed me with, in "unique ways"

To challenge the spirit of man was also my quest

To the degree in life it would not let me rest

So I strive to make a difference through the "written word"

Society gives me reason, purpose, and need to be heard

So I come as one "crying in the wilderness" "heralding"

Like the masses who goes "Christmas caroling"

I pressed on toward the mark

To awaken a spirit lost in the dark

To cultivate the "wheat" growing with the tares

For it's this plight that my soul bears

But more so, to open the eyes of the children of men

Before they are harvested by workers of sin

Maybe that man should look back at "The Poet" someday

And remember when I spoke I had something to say

Maybe at times it was about fifteen minutes of fame

But to "God" goes the "glory" just the same

For those who (know or) knew me best, always knew

It was "His will" I strove to do.

Well there's another effort made, another test of time recorded to create and epic creation of times and times gone by attempting to broaden your awareness, enlighten your mind, or free your spirit for as sure as "HE," "stands at the door and knocks," I come as "wisdom at the gate."

"For my main purpose was to lift "His" name in praise"...

"To make a difference through the written word"...

...For as always I come as "one crying in the wilderness, trying to open the eyes of the children of man, before they are "harvested" by minds of destruction"

"I AM THAT I AM"

Who am I...

I am every Father's desire and I encounter every Mother's sorrow

I am the reason you should train up a child in the way he should go

The reason you should vote

The reason you should help those who can't help themselves

I am the reason why you should reason

That except by the Grace of God there stands I I am that I am

I am the hope for tomorrow

Charles E. Peterson Sr.

"SUNSET"

Today although many "CYCLE OF LIFE," are transitioning rapidly before our eyes, we rarely filter through or receive the benefits gained from yesterday, or yesterday's pasted, that were set in place to prepare us for the challenges of today. That when found, understood, and incorporated into this walk of life, would indeed prepare us and often provide us with the wisdom needed for tomorrow. By causing us to venture back to our roots, questioning how we got here from there, or truly visualize the effects that each new road we travel or venture down is but one where those who made the paths of the past, sojourned. Maybe you don't get it, it's no longer about them nor actually about your children (to some degree), but it is "actually" all about you. About what you've learned from the "old warriors" of yesterday, that will help you to raise the children of tomorrow. It's all about how "the children of tomorrow" who are watching the example that "you and I" set today, will approach their test of time. So as we crisscross on the blood, sweat, and tears of the past, trying to make our mark on this day in time, remember that the crossroads that you encounter and venture down in whatever direction, may hold the key or keys to maintaining the,

"CYCLES OF LIFE,"
for the future generations.

Listen, can you hear "The Beat," (Boom bababoom bababoom bababoom ba) it's the heartbeat of a people, that's echoing, "those who reap the fruits of today, owe those who sowed the seeds of yesterday, to prepare a harvest, for the children of tomorrow," it's the Foundation and Rhythm of the:
"Cycles Of Life."

Charles E. Peterson Sr. The Poet

Remember the **"Sunsets,"** only to reveal the **"dawn"** of a "New Day." A **"Blank Page,"** on which to **"scribe."**

Made in the USA
Monee, IL
15 August 2023

40785855R00085